Twilight of Steam

Twilight of Steam

Written and Photographed
by
COLIN D. GARRATT

LONDON
BLANDFORD PRESS

First published 1972

ISBN 0 7137 0580 9

Colour section printed in 4-colour photogravure by D. H. Greaves Ltd, Scarborough. Text Computer Typeset in 9 point Baskerville, printed and bound by C. Tinling & Co. Ltd, London and Prescot

For my friend
Judy Warner

The author wishes to make acknowledgment to Agfa Gevaert Ltd, for the Agfacolor film used in the preparation of this book.

Foreword

It is an unalterable law of the universe that all forms of creation have, within themselves, defects that make inevitable their ultimate disappearance. The steam locomotive has proved to be no exception to this fundamental rule. It was unavoidable that the day should come when it went the way of the dinosaur and Imperial Rome. Those who loved the steam locomotive may accept this, but acceptance does nothing to reduce their regrets over the passing of one of the most fascinating of man's creations. Consolation is best found by doing something to keep the memory of the engines alive.

There are many ways in which the age of steam may continue as a living force in the minds of interested people and each method is valuable. Some are engaged in the preservation of actual locomotives or even complete railway lines; some are skilled builders of models; others keep memory alive by recalling past history through the written word. But perhaps the most popular activity of the steam locomotive enthusiast has been photography. Photography has long been a way of life for some of steam's most devoted followers, but never have the photographers been as active as during these final years leading up to the disappearance of steam from commercial service on the railways of the world.

As the years have passed, the photographer has had to adapt his art to the changing world. Before World War I a photographer could set up his tripod beside a main line and not move his position an inch. All he had to do was to reload his camera and press his shutter as each train came into view, and by the end of the day he would have collected a set of pictures of great variety. The trains themselves would have provided that variety. In more recent years, however, standardisation, nationalisation, modernisation and closures have all reduced it and photographers have had to find new viewpoints to add interest to their pictures. As the need for a different approach increased, photographic equipment progressed to keep pace with the changing demand. The more convenient roll film replaced the heavy glass plate, cameras became smaller and lighter, depth of focus improved but perhaps the greatest step forward of all was the rise of colour photography to a practical art form.

In recent years the reputation of Colin Garratt has been growing among the clubs and societies where railway enthusiasts meet. Combining, as he does, his technical knowledge of both colour photography and locomotives with the energy of youth, he has carried his art into a new dimension. His skilled use of colour, composition and form owes much to the master painters, for Colin Garratt uses his camera lens as an artist uses his brush.

This book is the first of a series dealing with 'The Last Steam Locomotives of the World' in which it is hoped to make use of recent advances in colour photography to present an exciting and vivid account of the final years of steam.

At this point in history, when interest in steam has never been greater, it is indeed the correct moment for such a series to be produced both as a work of art and as historical documentation of the world wide demise of steam. It seems particularly appropriate for an Englishman to travel the world, to record for a British publisher, the final years of a British invention which has been of great benefit to all mankind.

Colin Garratt regards the making of this series of books as something much more than a job of work. To him the recording of the final years of steam by colour photography is more than a profession, it is an act of faith. Enthusiasts of an older generation, proud of our own, relatively crude, black and white photographs of engines scrapped long before Colin was born, admire the way in which he has not accepted the end of steam as being final but rather has sought out such steam as remains. Not only has he shown that there remains more steam in this country than most people thought, but he has travelled far and intends to travel further still in pursuit of steam in other lands. Such effort deserves success and the attempt to combine the aesthetic and living qualities of the steam locomotive with its historical story is to be applauded. All true lovers of steam will wish this series well.

Leicester 2 March, 1972   John F. Clay

Introduction

I was immensely thrilled by the prospect of undertaking a series of books on the last steam locomotives of the world, but wondered for some time about the best method of approaching the task. After much thought, several basic requisites became apparent. Foremost was that the books should be in colour, for only by the use of colour do we see truth, while the illustrations needed to conjure up the living atmosphere of the subject and to preserve for all time the drama of the moment in which they were taken. I felt this to be especially important, as a large percentage of interest in steam engines is based upon emotionalism and aesthetics and therefore any serious documentation of the subject must take these factors into account. Accordingly, I have endeavoured, photographically, to convey as authentically as possible the vitality of Western Europe's steam engines as they enter their final years, while on the more practical side I have given details of the locomotives' history and working environment along with some account of my impressions and adventures when locating these engines. Thus a combination of Art, History and Adventure may be said to have been achieved, not because I profess to be a master of such diversities but simply because I felt that this would be the best method of presentation. No encyclopaedic pattern will be found within these pages, nor in those of succeeding books, but the culmination is intended to be a dramatic and truthful portrayal of the final days of steam power on the world's railways.

The systematists may criticise me for illustrating certain types of engine more than once but for this I make no apology, because although I have included a wide range of locomotive designs some of them do warrant more than one illustration. An obvious example is the several plates of Portuguese inside-cylinder 4–6–0s but these engines, apart from being extremely pleasing aesthetically, represent the lineage of a long past phase of locomotive design and deserve considerable coverage. Neither has it been my intention to adhere rigidly to strict geographical regions within each volume although each book should cover reasonably clearly defined areas.

Today the pursuit of steam locomotives is a painstaking and arduous task – certainly throughout most of Europe – for in Western Europe they are now relatively thin on the ground and, despite their being more numerous behind the Iron Curtain, the political situation in the communist countries renders the serious study of locomotives very hazardous. Even in the West, when engines are located, capturing them through a camera lens presents a new spate of difficulties for they can so easily elude the photographer because of the lack of suitable lighting, the wrong pictorial setting, incorrect colour balances or even a total absence of any visible smoke and steam – all vital elements which collectively constitute a worthwhile picture. When on various photographic locations at all hours of the day and night, I often think of the painter who, in the comfort of his studio, portrays his art largely as he wishes, whereas the photographer has thousands of miles to travel and innumerable environmental problems to overcome. But I would not change place with the painter, for a unique stimulation comes from the act of tracking down and filming these remnants of the steam age. It is strange to think of 'tracking them down', as this is a phrase more commonly used in connection with wild animal expeditions, and yet I have always felt that the vast interest in locomotives springs from some organic link with nature, for their immense animation seems to inspire in men the same feelings of awe and respect as do wild beasts. Furthermore, it is strange to realise that in exactly the same way as we have provided game reserves for the world's fast-diminishing wild beasts, so we have provided preserved lines for some steam engines. My metaphor with wild beasts becomes increasingly poignant as time progresses, for nowadays the sight of a steam engine rampaging across the landscape is intrinsically akin to some wild, if not pre-historic, creature.

I have endeavoured to capture in my colour plates what I have described elsewhere in the book as 'the elusive air of the authentic' and in so doing I hope to provide a valuable historical dimension. This is the driving force behind my expeditions – expeditions where we live and travel for weeks in converted road vehicles in order to achieve the utmost in mobility, which allows us to keep up with our quarry. Naturally the cost of these expeditions is high and an adventurous itinerary is the only way of gleaning the maximum value from them. Accordingly, meals and sleep tend to be fitted in around the steam locomotive workings. So often after finishing photography in the early hours of the morning I feel a necessity to be up before dawn to utilise the effects of the following morning's sunrise. Somehow, though, such is the consummate appeal of steam engines that one never gets tired, and it is my ardent hope that some of this appeal is communicated to you in the following pages.

All photography was undertaken on the Practica range of 35mm cameras using Tessar and Pancolar lenses.

Finally I must convey my warmest thanks to the following willing friends who have helped me in the preparation of this book: Horace Gamble, Bill Parkes, John F. Clay, David Thornhill and his excellent monthly publication *World Steam,* which is available from 124 Wendover Road, Aylesbury, Bucks., Gordon Caddy, F. W. Burnside, Joseph Gales, Peter Coton, A. Civil, Judith Hampton, Mrs M. E. Warner and Judy Warner.

September, 1971   Colin D. Garratt

The texts refer to a selection of locomotives from the following countries

Country	Railway company		Gauge
Great Britain	B.R.	British Railways	$4'\,8\frac{1}{2}''$
France	S.N.C.F.	Societé Nationale des Chemins de Fer Francais: French National Railways	$4'\,8\frac{1}{2}''$
West Germany	D.B.	Deutsche Bundesbahn: German Federal Railway	$4'\,8\frac{1}{2}''$

(After World War II the railways of Germany were divided and the pre-war title of Deutsche Reichsbahn (D.R.) was taken by the newly-formed East Germany, while West Germany's railways became the D.B. The initials D.R.B. have been used in the text to denote the pre-war German railways and thus differentiate them from the present day D.R.)

Austria	Ö.B.B.	Österreichischen Bundesbahnen: Austrian Federal Railways	$4'\,8\frac{1}{2}''$
Spain	R.E.N.F.E.	Red Nacional de los Ferrocarriles Espanõles: Spanish National Railways	$5'\,5\frac{13}{16}''$
Portugal	C.P.	Companhia Do Caminhos De Ferro Portugueses: Portuguese Railway Company	
		Broad	$5'\,5\frac{9}{16}''$
		Narrow (Metre)	$3'\,3\frac{3}{8}''$

11

1 **SMOKE, STEAM AND SPEED.** An O.B.B., Class 97 0–6–2T furiously blasts away from Erzberg with a loaded iron-ore train.

2 **B12s AND BOATS (1).** One of the C.P.'s Henschel inside-cylinder 4–6–0s, nicknamed B12s, approaches Pinhao with a mixed train from Regua.

3 **B12s AND BOATS (2).** A Porto-bound express accelerates away from Pinhao headed by a C.P. Henschel inside-cylinder 4–6–0.

4 **SILHOUETTE AT SUNRISE.** The silhouette of a R.E.N.F.E. oil-fired 141F 2–8–2 in contrast with the rising sun at Castejon.

5 **WESTBOUND DEPARTURE.** B.R. West Country Class, *Woolacombe*, leaves Basingstoke with a York–Bournemouth express.

6 **TWILIGHT AT NÜRNBERG.** A freight pulls heavily out of the yards at Nürnberg behind a D.B. 050 2–10–0.

7 **GETTING TO GRIPS (1).** One of the surviving D.B. 038 4–6–0s works up a spanking pace out of Horb with a Stuttgart line train.

8   **GETTING TO GRIPS (2)**. A D.B. 050 2–10–0 bursts under the girders at Horb with a morning train for Tübingen.

9 **THROUGH CAVERNS MEASURELESS.** One of the C.P.'s Metre Gauge, Kessl

—6–0Ts of 1886, threads its way through the suburbs of Porto with a train from Fafe.

10 **VETERAN OF VERDUN.** A scene in the ancient roundhouse at Verdun with an S.N.C.F. 140C 2–8–0.

11 **ENGINES OF WAR.** Two ex-German Krieglokomotiven amid the gloomy portals of Vienna Nord shed. O.B.B., Class 52, 2–10–0.

12 **DUST AND DERELICTION.** A withdrawn R.E.N.F.E. 241F 4-8-2 lies in the abandoned depot at Lerida.

13 **141Fs ON PARADE.** Four R.E.N.F.E. 141F, 2-8-2s await their next turn of duty at Castejon.

14 **PORTUGUESE ELEGANCE.** Detailed study of a C.P. Metre Gauge 2–4–6–0T Henschel Mallet.

15 **MISTY EVENING.** An O.B.B., Class 97 0–6–2T pauses at Präbichl before proceeding down to Vordernberg with a loaded train.

16 **PONFERRADA NOCTURNE (1).** One of the P.V.'s Macosa 2–6–0s simmers on night duty at Ponferrada.

17 **PONFERRADA NOCTURNE (2)**. P.V. Baldwin 2–6–2T, *Arana Lupardo*, in repose at Ponferrada shed.

18 **WITH THE RISING SUN**. . . . . . a D.B. 038 4–6–

rms along the Stuttgart line with a train from Horb.

19 **ACTION ON THE CLIFFTOPS.** . . . . . as *Stanley*, a Hunslet 0–6–0ST, shunts at Haig Colliery, Whitehaven.

20 **CONFRONTATION.** A peasant lady waits for a C.P. Metre Gauge Henschel 2–4–6–0T Mallet to pass as it approaches Vila Real with a Corgo line train.

121 **WATERSMEET.** A C.P. inside-cylinder Henschel 4–6–0 crosses the River Tua at Tua, with the River Douro in the background.

22 **PORTO SUBURBAN.** One of the C.P.'s Metre Gauge 0–4–4–0T Mallets gets into its stride past Senhora da Hora with a Porto-bound train.

23　**A HAPPENING AT CASTEJON.** One of the massive R.E.N.F.E. 242Fs in good fettle at Castejon.

24　**BEASTS AT LARGE (1).** In contrast with the ever watchful eagle, a D.B. 044 2–10–0 plunges into Cochem tunnel with freight for Koblenz.

25 **SIGNALS AT SENHORA (1).** A lovely Henschel 2–8–2T of the C.P. Metre Gauge pulls away from Senhora da Hora with a Povoa–Porto train.

26 **SIGNALS AT SENHORA (2).** With steam shut off, a C.P. Metre Gauge Kessler 2–6–0T ambles into Senhora da Hora with a train from Porto.

27 **AMONGST THE PEAKS.** An O.B.B. 97 0–6–2T makes a labour

scent between Erzberg and Präbichl with a loaded ironstone train.

28 **WOODLAND STUDIES (1).** The Midday train from Aveiro–Sernada headed by a
C.P. Metre Gauge Orenstein-Koppel 2–6–0T.

29 **WOODLAND STUDIES (2).** One of the elusive C.P. Henschel Pacifics is caught highwheeling through the woods at Lousada with an express for Moncao.

30 **WOODLAND STUDIES (3).** A C.P. Metre Gauge Henschel 2–4–6–0T Mallet storms the spiral out of Sernada with an Esphino line train.

31 **INDUSTRIAL STUDIES (1).** Night-time at Haig Colliery with Hunslet 0–6–0ST, *Stanley*.

32 **INDUSTRIAL STUDIES (2).** An R.S.H. 0–4–0ST operates a night turn at Leicester Power Station.

33 **SHADES OF EVENING.** Giesl fitted Hunslet 0–6–0ST, *Stanley*, blends with the evening seascape at Whitehaven.

34 **ONE FOR THE CAPITAL.** B.R. Merchant Navy, *Aberdeen Commonwealth*, races through Winchester with a London-bound express.

35 **GOLDEN PRODUCE.** *Caerphilly*, a Kitson 0–6–0ST, at work on the Storefield Ironstone system, Northamptonshire.

INSPECTION. Two R.E.N.F.E. 141F 2–8

...ceive last minute attentions at Castejon depot.

37 **TERMINAL.** A C.P. Metre Gauge Henschel 0–4–4–0T Mallet confronts the buffer stops at Porto Trindade station.

38 **SUNDOWN AT MIRANDA.** An R.E.N.F.E. 141F 2–8–2 blushes at the sight of the westering sun in Miranda depot.

39 **AMID PASTURES SERENE (1).** Giesl fitted Hunslet 0–6–0ST, *Warspite*, storms away from Lowca exchange sidings near Workington.

40 **AMID PASTURES SERENE (2).** *Amazon*, a Hunslet designed 0–6–0ST with standard chimney, at Lowca Colliery.

41 **AMID PASTURES SERENE (3).** Hunslet designed 0–6–0ST, *Amazon*, darkens the summer skies at Lowca.

42 **DOURO VALLEY.** A C.P. Henschel 2–6–4T at the head of an Easter special from Porto-Régua.

43 **SPANISH VINTAGE.** Ex-A.G.L., N.O.R.T.E. and R.E.N.F.E. 0–6–0, *Eslava*, now owned by the Minas de Aller complex, Ujó.

44 **SHADES OF VERMEER.** One of the handsome C.P. North British 2–8–0s dominates the turntable at Porto Contumil depot.

45 **ALSASUA BOUND.** One of the R.E.N.F.E.
Castejon–Alsasua freight.

nificent 242Fs prepares to work a

46 **HOLIDAY EXTRA.** An ex-M.Z.A., R.E.N.F.E. 240F 4–8–0 struggles out of Salamanca with a heavy holiday relief train.

47   **WITH A MENACING AIR.** A diminutive C.P. Metre Gauge Kessler 0–6–0T engages
itself in shunting activities at Tua.

48 **METRE GAUGE VIADUCTS (1).** A Chaves-bound train crosses Tanha Viaduct behind a C.P. Henschel 2–4–6–0T Mallet.

49 **METRE GAUGE VIADUCTS (2).** With Sernada to the rear, a C.P. Orenstein-Koppel 2–6–0T crosses the viaduct with a mixed train to Aveiro.

50 **VOLCANO ON THE MOVE.** The sole surviving C.P. Schwarzkopf 4-cylinder compound 2–8–0 darkens the woods as it heads eastwards from Ermida.

51 MAJESTY ON THE MOVE. One of the beautiful C.P. Henschel 4–6–0s raises the dawn echoes as it slams out of Régua with a mixed train to Pochino.

52 **TROUBLE AT THE POWER STATION.** An R.S.H. 0–4–0ST brigh

night skies at Leicester Power Station as it attempts to lift a heavy coal train.

53 **CONTRASTS IN FORM.** *Bilbao*, a 5 ft. 6 in. Turon-built 2–4–0T, shunts the yard at Turon, whilst a less fortunate sister, a 600 mm. 0–4–0T, lies derelict.

DIGNITY AND IMPUDENCE. *Roker*, an R.S.H. 0–4–0CT, looking a little severe at Doxford's Shipyard, Sunderland.

55 **TRINDADE BY NIGHT.** A C.P. Metre Gauge Henschel 0–4–4–0T Mallet against the darkened city at Porto Trindade station.

56　**NIGHT FIRE.** An R.E.N.F.E. 141F 2–8–2 enlivens the yards at Salamanca with a passing freight.

57　**NIGHT TURN.** One of the C.P.'s Schwarzkopf-built 2–8–0s raises steam at Régua.

58 **4-6-0s—HENSCHEL STYLE (1).** A C.P. Henschel inside-cylinder 4-6-0 ambles across the viaduct at Tua with an eastbound freight.

59 **4-6-0s—HENSCHEL STYLE (2).** With the hamlet of Tua in the background, a C.P. Henschel outside-cylinder 4–6–0 heads a westbound mixed train over the viaduct.

BEASTS AT LARGE (2). The Kaiser Wilhelm tunnel at Cochem a

host to a D.B. Class 023 2–6–2 on a Saarbrücken–Koblenz passenger train.

61 **ARRIVAL FROM THE BORDER** (**1**). An R.E.N.F.E. 141F 2–8–2 pulls into Salamanca with an express from the Portuguese border at Fuentes de Onoro.

62 **ARRIVAL FROM THE BORDER** (**2**). An ex-M.Z.A., R.E.N.F.E. 240F 4–8–0 prepares to leave Salamanca with a night express to Medina.

63 **DEPARTURE TO THE COAST.** The night train from Sernada-Aveiro leaves behind a C.P. Metre Gauge Orenstein-Koppel 2–6–0T.

64　**BREAK FOR REFRESHMENT.** Spanish Industrial 2–4–0T *Bilbao* takes a break between duties on the Turon Colliery system.

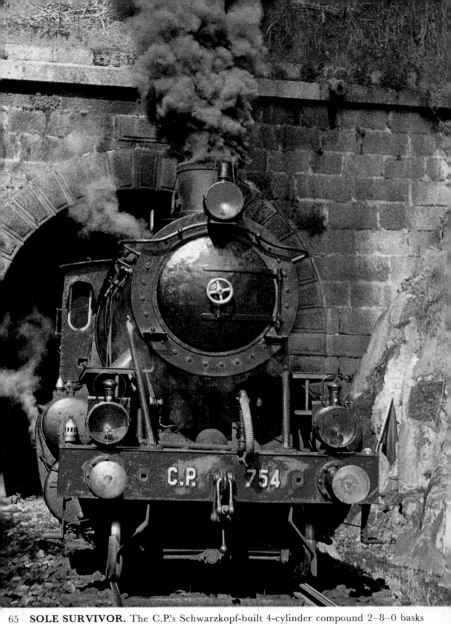

65 **SOLE SURVIVOR.** The C.P.'s Schwarzkopf-built 4-cylinder compound 2–8–0 basks in the sunlight at Ermida tunnel.

66 **THROUGH THE ALPINE STILLNESS.** . . . . . an O.B.B. 97 0–6–2T clanks a string
of empty waggons along the iron mountain-line.

67 **VAPOUR.** Two O.B.B. 97 0–6–2Ts, storm the rack section between Platten Tunnel and Präbichl with ironstone for Vordernberg.

68 **NIGHT EXPRESS.** An ex-M.Z.A., R.E.N.F.E. 2

—0 prepares to leave Salamanca with a train to Medina.

69   **TRAINS AND TRAMS.** One of the famous Porto trams trundles overhead as a C.P. Metre Gauge, Henschel 0–4–4–0T Mallet simmers between turns of duty at Trindade.

70 **UNDER THE CITY.** C.P. Metre Gauge 0–4–4–0T Mallet busily shunts stock at Trindade station, Porto.

71 **AUSTRIAN INTERLUDE.** One of the ancient O.B.B., 91 Class, 2-cylinder compound
2–6–0Ts, prepares to leave Neuberg with a branch train to Murzzuschlag.

72 **LONG HAUL.** With the famous viaduct in the background, a C.P. Henschel 4–6–0
arrives at Ferradosa with a heavy freight train.

73 TREASURES OF PORTO. An ancient C.P. Metre Gauge Kessler 2–6–0T climbs out of Porto with a train to Fafe.

74 **EARLY DUTY AT PALLION (1).** Doxford's R.S.H. 0–4–0CT, *Millfield*, faces a
wintery dawn at Pallion Shipyard, Sunderland.

75 **EARLY DUTY AT PALLION (2).** *Millfield*, an R.S.H. 0–4–0CT, prepares for the day's duties at Pallion shed.

76 **INTERRUPTED TRANQUILITY.** A C.P. Metre Gauge Orenstein-Koppel 2–6–

turbs the silence as it crosses the River Vouga at Sernada with an Aveiro train.

77 **TWO IN TANDEM.** Two C.P. Tanks: an S.L.M. 2–6–4 and a Henschel 2–8–4, head a northbound train from Porto Campanha.

78 **STUDIES IN SILHOUETTE (1).** Afternoon activities at Lowca Washery performed by Hunslet 0–6–0ST, *Warspite*.

79 **STUDIES IN SILHOUETTE (2).** The C.P.'s 4-cylinder compound 2–8–0 makes heavy weather as it approaches Régua with freight for the Spanish border.

80 **DEPARTURES FROM REGUA (5 ft. 6 in.).** A C.P. Henschel 4–6–0 gets into its stride with an evening train for Tua.

81 DEPARTURES FROM REGUA (METRE). A Henschel 2–4–6–0T Mallet pulls
away with a Corgo line train for Chaves.

82 **PAST SNOWY PEAKS.** . . . . . A P.V. Krauss 2–6–0 heads northwards near Torino with coal empties for Villablino.

83 . . . . . **THROUGH VALLEYS REMOTE.** The P.V. Krauss 2–6–0 continues its journey northwards to Villablino through the picturesque Sil Valley.

84 **FIERY PHANTOM.** A Schwarzkopf 2–8–0 of the C

...ds a touch of animation to the freight yards at Régua.

85 **RURAL SPLENDOUR.** An O.B.B. Class 91 2–6–0T, at work on the scenic branch
from Murzzuschlag to Neuberg.

86 **METRE GAUGE JOYS (1).** A C.P. Orenstein-Koppel Metre Gauge 2–6–0T leaves Sernada for Aveiro.

87 **METRE GAUGE JOYS (2).** One of the original batch of Henschel Metre Gauge 2–8–2Ts of the C.P., heads up towards Viseu from Sernada.

STUDIES IN BLACK AND UMBER (1). Some full-blooded activity occurring at Salamanca with an ex-M.Z.A., R.E.N.F.E. 240F 4–8–0.

89 **STUDIES IN BLACK AND UMBER (2).** A handsome C.P. Metre Gauge Henschel 0–4–4–0T Mallet at Trindade.

90 **JOURNEY'S END.** One of the O.B.B.'s splendid 78 Class, 4–6–4Ts lying derelict at Amstetten.

91 **SUPREME EFFORT.** A Giesl-fitted O.B.B. 97 0–6–2T fights its way over the rack section on the long haul up to Präbichl summit from Vordernberg.

TRIUMPHS OF ENGINEERING. The famous viaduct o

Douro at Ferradosa blends well with a C.P. Henschel 4–6–0.

93 **IRONSTONE MEMORIES (1).** Dwarfed by the Walking Dragline, Hunslet 16 in. 0–6–0ST, *Jacks Green*, waits to leave the pit face at Nassington with a loaded train.

94 **IRONSTONE MEMORIES (2).** Hunslet 16 in. 0–6–0ST, *Ring Haw*, takes a loaded train along the gullet at Nassington.

95 **PRUSSIAN SURVIVOR.** One of the few remaining D.B. 078 4–6–4Ts enters Rottweil with a train for Villingen.

96 **WEYMOUTH BOUND.** B.R. Merchant Navy Class, *Elder Dempster Lines*, receives the right away from Wareham.

97 **FOGGY DAY AT CRANFORD.** Bagnall 0–6–0ST, *Cranford No 2*, storms through the Northamptonshire countryside on the Cranford ironstone system near Kettering.

98 **VIBRANCE.** A pair of D.B. 044 2–10–0s make a vigorous assault on the climb out of Bullay with a southbound hopper train.

99 **DEEP IN THE DEPTHS.** . . . . . . of Vienna Nord depot, an O.B.B. 93 Class 2–8–2T reposes amid the gloom.

100 **ACROSS FALLOW PLAINS.** An ex-M.Z.A., R.E.N.F.E. 240F 4–8–0 charges west
wards against the stormclouds with a **Portugal-bound** freight.

Descriptions to the Coloured
Illustrations

Clun Castle – Castle Class 4–6–0   **Front endpaper**

Every revolution possesses its heroes, and *Clun Castle* was
the hero of the lost cause of steam in the mid 1960s. During
those dark days of steam's run down in Britain this engine
survived all her sisters to become one of the last stalwarts in a
diminishing era – a solitary star on a storm-swept night.
These were the days when Britain's steam engines were as
begrimed, clanking skeletons, shorn of all adornments and
eking out a living death. Almost to the very end, *Clun Castle*
was resplendently maintained in her attractive green livery
for use on farewell specials in many parts of the country and
it seemed incomprehensible that she would ever be withdrawn. Millions of people flocked to the lineside to see her
on these runs, such as the last steam train run from Paddington or the famous specials, along with *Pendennis Castle,* to
mark the ending of expresses between Paddington and
Chester. Such is the magic of steam, a magic which becomes
personified in types like the ex-G.W.R. Castles; their dignity
of appearance and excellence of performance have assured
them a leading place in British locomotive history, for they
were masterpieces in every respect.

Of all *Clun Castle's* exploits perhaps the most famous was
her working of the last steam train out of Paddington, a
commemorative special put on by British Rail Western
Region, who in their publicity on the occasion declared:
'The public are respectfully informed that the last steam train
from Paddington will be worked by locomotive number
7029, *Clun Castle,* departing from Platform five at 9.18 am on
Saturday, 27 November, 1965, and travelling to Swindon,
Bristol, Gloucester and other contiguous places.'

I was on that train, and the atmosphere at Paddington
before departure was unbelievably sad; hundreds of people
came to the station to witness the event and pay their last
respects. To many of them the Great Western Railway had   109

been a part of their lives. Certainly, from a locomotive viewpoint, it had been a railway of high standards and fine traditions, most of its top locomotives in their respective generations having been widely recognised as outstanding. Now under B.R. that tradition was to pass for ever. With a heart-rending cry from *Clun's* whistle we set out for the west and it seemed as if London itself had momentarily stopped to salute the event. An endless sea of faces lined the route and to say that many were tear-stained is no exaggeration, for here was something that really mattered to people, and its enforced removal was for them an event of deep sadness.

Our day with the big green engine was, despite the occasion, a real adventure. The autumn sunshine caught her shining brasswork, causing it to flash myriad tones of gold, and her clouds of white, puffy smoke drifted lazily across the soft Wiltshire countryside, only to change to storm-clouds as we forged our way up Sapperton Bank. Her bell-like whistle echoed across the rolling downs, blessing the landscape with a delicate touch of animation, and causing children to start up from their play and run gleefully towards the approaching train. *Clun Castle* was not in good form that day but it hardly mattered, as for over forty years her breed had more than proved itself. At Swindon, on the return journey, links with steam were severed. It was planned to whisk us back to Paddington behind two English Electric type 3 diesels in 60 minutes for the 77.3 miles, thus heralding the new age, and beating the fastest booked time of the pre-war, Castle-hauled *Cheltenham Flyer Express* of 65 minutes over the same stretch – although one Castle once ran the distance in $56\frac{1}{2}$ minutes, a start-to-stop average of 82 m.p.h.! After a devastatingly fast run, which demonstrated to all of us how thrilling the *Cheltenham Flyer* schedule must have been, the two diesels failed to make the grade. All the way up from Swindon, tension had been rising on the train as every coach had its hard core of timers, many with logs of old *Cheltenham Flyer* runs, and our progress was called out every mile or so. It was truly an emotionally-charged occasion, and when it became obvious that the diesels had fallen short, cheers rang out throughout the train. After all, this was *Clun Castle's* day and although we were keyed up for a fast run, none of us wanted the old Castle schedule to be beaten. I forget the exact timing but we ran into Paddington in just a shade over 65 minutes.

The illustration depicts *Clun Castle* racing through Newton Harcourt, south of Leicester, with a railtour in 1964. Although the Castles first appeared in 1923, it was not until May, 1950 that *Clun Castle* was built, beginning life at Swindon Works as lot No. 375. Accordingly, she was always a British Railways engine although built to the old formula with only a few detail differences. The most noticeable of these was the double chimney, fitted in July, 1962. In the same year as the photograph was taken, the engine achieved fame by hauling a 265-ton train from Plymouth to Bristol, whereupon 96 m.p.h. was attained on Wellington Bank, 90 m.p.h. maintained for twelve miles continuously and ten minutes cut off the 72-minute schedule between Exeter and Bristol.

The news of *Clun Castle's* preservation created a milestone in preservation history, and today thousands of people enjoy seeing her in resplendently preserved form at the Standard Gauge Steam Trust's depot at Tyseley in Birmingham, where the engine is steamed on certain occasions along with other important locomotives. Upon seeing *Clun,* or in fact any of the other three preserved Castles, my mind runs back over the history of the class when the first one, 4073 *Caerphilly Castle,* emerged from Swindon in August, 1923. No less than twenty-seven years later the final example of the class appeared and was named *Swindon* in commemoration of it being the last Great Western passenger engine to be constructed at those famous works. This engine brought the final total of Castles to 171 engines. The type represented the principal express motive-power of the G.W.R. for over forty years. Always record breakers, one recalls *Dynevor Castle's* exploits in 1935 when it raced over the 226 miles between Plymouth and Paddington in 218 minutes, or more recently the brilliant performances with the *Bristolian,* once Britain's fastest train, which was frequently worked up to speeds of 95–100 m.p.h. during its 118-mile dash between London and Bristol. Other named trains operated by Castles were: *The Torbay Express, The Cathedrals Express, The Royal Duchy,* and *The South Wales Pullman.*

Apart from *Clun,* other preserved Castles are *Caerphilly Castle* and *Pendennis Castle*; the former resides in Kensington Science Museum whilst the latter is well maintained by the Great Western Society at their Didcot headquarters. A fourth example is to be preserved having recently been retrieved successfully from the locomotive scrapyards at Barry. *Clun Castle,* in common with her sisters, has the following specifications: 4 cylinders 16" × 26", driving wheel diameter 6' 8½", boiler pressure 225 lb per sq in, grate area 29½ sq ft and a tractive effort of 31,625 lb. Her coal and water capacity are 6 tons and 4,000 gallons respectively and total weight in working order is 127 tons. At the time of *Clun's* withdrawal from traffic, it was estimated that she had run over 666,000 miles in her sixteen years of active service – a continuous average of 800 miles per week. So, for a period, ended the saga of the Castles but let us hope that their story is not yet completed. *Clun Castle,* along with *Pendennis,* is still in excellent running order and if the present B.R. ban on steam specials is lifted, she will have an opportunity to show the flamboyance of her former years and once again green, copper-capped engines will amble through the English countryside with that grace of movement unique to Great Western engines. How much richer our environment would be for such á sight, and how much pleasure would be given to so many! In Britain we still pride ourselves upon our democracy and tolerance and it seems totally out of character for such a ban to remain for so long. Surely one day a more enlightened attitude must prevail and when this occurs, *Clun Castle* may head yet another revolution. In fact at the time of writing, news has just reached me of sister engine, ex-G.W.R. *King George V*, running experimentally over B.R. metals, and this event could herald a new attitude from B.R. towards Britain's preserved steam engines. Although at present no press release on this matter has been issued, Britain's enthusiasts await further news with bated breath.

Ö.B.B. 97 Class 0–6–2T   Pl. 1, 15, 27, 66, 67, 91

Undoubtedly one of the most fascinating steam-operated lines in the world is the Erzberg, perhaps more popularly known as the 'Iron Mountain Railway'. Situated in a comparatively remote mountain district at the eastern end of the Austrian Alps, the function of this standard-gauge line is to convey iron-ore from the Erzberg, a 2,400 ft high mountain of solid iron-ore, to the steelworks at Donawitz, and the end of the line at Vordernberg facilitates this by connecting with the Ö.B.B.'s electrified main line.

Authorised in 1888, the line was registered primarily for iron-ore traffic, but provision was also made for a passenger service for the local inhabitants and to this day three return passenger trains travel the complete length of the line, from Vordernberg through to Eisenerz, daily. Building the line through such a treacherous mountain district presented innumerable problems and although only $12\frac{1}{2}$ miles in length, the line was not opened until 1891 and then only at a cost which greatly exceeded all estimates. In 1893 the Erzberg line was incorporated into the Imperial Royal Austrian State Railway system as a result of which it is now a part of the Ö.B.B.

One of the many fascinating aspects of this railway is its use of both 'rack and adhesion' traction. Much of the $12\frac{1}{2}$-mile route has a ruling gradient of 1 in 14 and over these sections the Abt system of rack operation is employed. Shortly after leaving Vordernberg, 2,525 ft above sea level, the rack system comes into operation for the five-mile climb to the summit at Präbichl, 3,952 ft above sea level. From

Präbichl the line commences a seven-mile descent to Eisen-erz, 2,269 ft above sea level. The majority of this section is rack-operated with the exception of Platten Tunnel which is one mile in length; through the tunnel the gradient relaxes to a mere 1 in 50! The steepest adhesion gradient, 1 in 38, occurs between Eisenerz and Krumpental. Erzberg lies approximately half-way between Präbichl and Eisenerz and, accordingly, iron-ore can be despatched in either direction. The ore is either transported over the rack to Vordernberg or via an electrically-operated tramway to Eisenerz, whereupon it is conveyed on the Ö.B.B.'s electrified main line either northwards to Linz, or round to Donawitz via Selzthal. The accompanying map will add greater clarity to the above paragraph.

It was suggested, upon completion of the Ö.B.B.'s Eisenerz–Hieflau–Selzthal–Donawitz electrification, that all iron-ore might be despatched this way, thereby dispensing with the rack line. Erzberg to Donawitz via the rack is only some 19 miles, whereas via Selzthal it is nearer 80 miles but, as surprising as it may seem, a case was presented, based on economics, to transfer all traffic over the longer route. Fortunately this plan was not adopted – to all railway

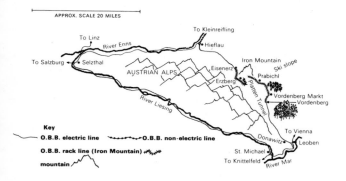

113

lovers' relief – and it appears that the rack line has every prospect of continuing for many years to come.

The line's original locomotives, supplied in 1890, were these splendid 0–6–2, 4-cylinder Rack/Adhesion Tank engines. They were delivered from the Floridsdorf works of Wiener Lokomotivfabrik A.G. Building continued up to 1908, by which time a total of 18 were in existence. Fourteen of these survive today, and they form the principal source of power for both mineral and passenger traffic. This class now represents the oldest locomotives in service on today's Ö.B.B.

These engines use simple expansion for both rack and adhesion mechanisms, possessing separate regulators but having combined reversing gear. To facilitate entry onto the Abt rack sections, the locomotives have geared to their rack wheels a red and white 'target', which rotates in time with the rack wheels; thus by opening the rack regulator so that the target can be seen to rotate in time with the adhesion exhaust beats, a smooth transition occurs. These 0–6–2Ts have proved themselves to be remarkably successful and are able to haul loads of 110 tons unassisted over the 1 in 14 gradients. Many, although I am glad to say not all, have been modernised by the addition of Giesl Ejectors.

In 1912 the Austrian State Railway's Chief Mechanical Engineer, Herr Gölsdorf, designed some marvellous 0–12–0 tank engines in order to increase the line's capacity. Three of these engines were built enabling the maximum load for an unassisted locomotive to be increased to 160 tons. Although an 0–12–0T is seemingly a strange design for so sinuous a route, considerable side-play was arranged in the 1st, 5th and 6th axles. Classified 197, these three engines still remain in service although they are primarily confined to shunting duties.

Over the next 30 years motive power on the line remained unchanged until the advent of World War II. This inevitably led to a vast increase in the demand for iron-ore and after Germany's occupation of Austria, the then Deutsche Reichsbahn, D.R.B., designed two giant 2–12–2 tank engines. These monsters were put into traffic in 1941 and they had a nominal tractive effort, at 75 per cent boiler pressure, of no less than 110,000 lb. Known as the 297 Class, these engines were built by Floridsdorf and proved themselves capable of hauling 400 tons over the 1 in 14 inclines at 9 m.p.h.! Unfortunately, they were too heavy and some strengthening of the track would have been necessary to absorb the thrust when working at full power. This was never carried out and upon the decreased post-war production of iron-ore they were withdrawn from service, although one of them is stored at Vordernberg awaiting eventual display in the Austrian

Railway Museum – and a highly worthwhile exhibit it will be! In fact the Austrians intend eventually to preserve both a 97 and a 197, the locomotives having already been earmarked; thus a permanent record of the line's motive power will be maintained.

All the Erzberg's locomotives are simples, each having two separate two-cylinder engines, one set driving the adhesion wheels and the other the cogged rack wheels. The leading dimensions of Class 97 are: cylinders (4) two adhesion $18\frac{3}{4}''$ × $19\frac{1}{2}''$ and two rack $16\frac{1}{2}''$ × $17\frac{3}{4}''$, driving wheels 3′ $4\frac{1}{2}''$ diameter, boiler pressure 156 lb per sq in, grate area 24 sq ft, and rack wheels of 2′ 3″ diameter. The class is not superheated.

Situated at Vordernberg are the locomotive sheds and works. In addition to the thrice-daily passenger trains to Eisenerz, a shuttle service is maintained between Vordernberg and Vordernberg Markt, $1\frac{1}{4}$ miles away, although the latest news is that a diesel has been tested on this duty. Normally, both empty and loaded iron-ore trains have a locomotive at each end. Sometimes, however, the returning loaded trains split into two halves between Erzberg and the summit at Präbichl, where they are reunited for transit down the rack to Vordernberg, again with one locomotive at each end.

As the relevant colour plates indicate, the scenery is truly magnificent, and a journey over the line by passenger train is a wonderful experience – especially when the trains are hauled by 80-year-old 0–6–2Ts. There is something about the Erzberg line that fires one with a feeling of adventure, because unobtrusively hidden among these Austrian Alps lies this steam paradise. It is an adventure all the more authentic for the line not being in any way a tourist attraction. Here is all the grime and glamour of steam power, with that special vintage touch. To stand on the mountainside between Vordernberg and Präbichl watching a procession of empty trains storming up the 1 in 14 is an unforgettable experience; the 0–6–2Ts' pounding rhythms echo and reverberate across the mountains, providing a poignant contrast to the alpine stillness.

C.P. Inside Cylinder 4–6–0 Nos 281–286

Pl. 2, 3, 21, 51, 58, 72, 80, 92

These lovely engines, which British enthusiasts have nicknamed 'B12s' owing to their similarity with the Holden ex-Great Eastern Railway 4–6–0s, are the curvaceous sisters of the C.P.'s 1913 4–6–0s discussed on page 169. To me they provide one of the cornerstones in the aesthetics of steam-engine design, and that is an almost indefinable combination of gracefulness and starkness. They are most commonly likened to the B12s but I find a 'London and North Western' air about them, for they more than superficially resemble that railway's 'Prince of Wales' Class 4–6–0s. Whatever one's feelings about them they are period pieces from a long vanished era of steam design and upon making my first acquaintance with the type in the summer of 1970 I found them to be a vivid reincarnation of a style of engine which I remember so well from my early boyhood days. The curvaceousness of the design is its predominant characteristic, and it may be seen in the chimney, smokebox saddle, bogie wheel guards, running plate, round topped firebox and cab design; all features which enable these engines to stand out imposingly against the Douro Valley Line's jagged ruggedness.

The class was delivered as a series of six engines in 1910 from Henschel of Germany for the S.S. division of the Portuguese State Railways and passed into C.P. ownership in 1927 (see page 159). All are based at Régua for operations on the Douro Valley Line with the exception of one engine which is stored at Vila Nova de Gaia. Early in 1971 one was fully overhauled in the C.P. works at Entroncamento and thus created a favourable sign of the class's retention for a year or two yet. They have 2 cylinders of $20\frac{1}{2}'' \times 25\frac{1}{2}''$, driving wheels of 5' 1" diameter, a grate area of 31 sq ft and a tractive effort of 22,507 lb, whilst their total weight in working order is 115 tons.

As this class of engine is associated with the Douro Valley, a few comments on the route itself might be timely. From Porto Campanhã the Minho/Douro lines follow the same route for $5\frac{1}{2}$ miles to Ermesinde, whereupon the latter diverges due east and climbs towards the Douro Valley until it reaches Pala; here it joins the River Douro which it then follows through to the Spanish frontier. For long stretches, the line battles its way through gorge, the principal stations being situated at points where side valleys merge with the Douro, and running through these are metre gauge feeder lines: the map on page 160 shows their exact location. The line ends at Barca d'Alva, 125 miles from Porto, and after crossing the border it continues to Salamanca. Construction began from Ermesinde in 1875 and the line was completed to the Spanish frontier by 1887. At Ferradosa, east of Tua, the line crosses onto the Douro's south bank via the magnificent Ferradosa Viaduct, a steel structure almost $\frac{1}{4}$ of a mile long. This structure, set deep in the valley, is awe inspiring and plate nos 72 and 92 show it along with one of the 4–6–0s under discussion. Owing to weight restrictions, no C.P. diesels are permitted east of Régua so that the portion of line from there to the border is entirely steam worked, excepting a daily railcar working from Salamanca.

When in the valley, I often base myself at one of the metre-gauge feeder points, usually Régua or Tua, and thus savour the delights of two entirely different steam-worked systems on mixed-gauge track. But as much as this I enjoy the valley for its unparalleled tranquillity. One can explore the line and spend a day alongside a favourite tunnel or bridge, possibly not seeing a soul all day. Few roads pass through the valley and consequently no tourists infiltrate into the area; thus in this fortress of solitude one is alone with nature. The sparseness of traffic is supplemented for me by the sight and sound of many birds, perhaps a gliding hawk, and I become lost in the wonders of existence until the distant cry of a chime whistle summons my awareness to the approach of a Henschel 4–6–0 – a whistle, incidentally, that would do justice to a Gresley A4! The valley and its engines have completely captivated me; the friendliness and warmth of the engine crews, a swig of wine on the footplate or perhaps the invitation to a glass of port in a lineside village, for here in the heart of the Port country the folk are proud to hand a glass of their produce to an English traveller. The port with its fine vintage and quality gives a perfect edge to days spent in the valley; an edge to which the B12s add a final touch of magic, and I hope that some of the beauty of these engines and the terrain amid which they work has been captured on the colour plates, for I have tried hard to portray them as I felt them.

R.E.N.F.E. 141F Class 2–8–2   Pl. 4, 13, 36, 38, 56, 61

By far the most common steam engines in Spain are these standard mixed-traffic locomotives which were built for the R.E.N.F.E from 1953–1960. The 2–8–2 type had previously been used in Spain by the N.O.R.T.E. but the R.E.N.F.E., realising its all-round usefulness, adopted it as a standard. Within two years of their introduction, 125 141Fs had been built and these, in line with Spanish practice, were divided into five orders of twenty-five, the first of which came from the North British Loco. Co. of Glasgow, whilst the other four batches were assigned to the Spanish builders of Macosa, Maquinista, Euskalduna and Babcock & Wilcox. All further construction was undertaken in Spain, although 100 of the Spanish-built engines were assembled from parts built by the North British Loco. Co., and by 1960, when the final eight were delivered from Euskalduna, the class totalled 240 engines.

The 141Fs have proved themselves to be exceptionally capable machines and may be found throughout all steam-worked areas of the R.E.N.F.E. As an all round, general purpose design, built in the dusk of the steam age, they remind one of the S.N.C.F. 141Rs, and I always feel that visually the two types have much in common, although the 141Rs are decidedly more rugged machines. All earlier 141Fs possessed single Kylala blast pipes and were coal-fired, but the final 117, delivered from 1954 onwards, were built as oil-burners with double chimneys; although two members of the class did manage to acquire Giesl ejectors!

All surviving Spanish steam engines are oil-burners and the earlier coal-burning 141Fs were either converted or withdrawn. This rapid conversion to oil-burning was facilitated by the R.E.N.F.E.'s drastic run down of steam which took place during the 1960s. How drastic this run down was may be seen by the fact that as recently as 1967 over fifty per cent of R.E.N.F.E. traffic was steam-operated whereas now it is considerably less than ten per cent. The reason for this conversion to oil-firing is the unsuitability of Spain's coal for use on locomotives: much of it is small and only suitable for main-line use when compressed into brickettes. These burn rapidly and allow much of the fuel to disappear up the chimney only partly burnt. Accordingly, an oil-burning policy was embarked upon to avoid the threefold problem of poor combustion, dirt and higher cost. During this transformation period all oil-burners were classified with an F, but since full implementation of the scheme this has become superfluous and is now being dropped. The building of the final 117 141Fs as oil-burners was in accordance with this scheme.

A distinctive feature of the 141Fs, which may be noted from the colour plates, is the large electric lights placed in front of their chimneys. Other fittings include feed water heaters. The leading dimensions of the class are: 2 cylinders $22\frac{1}{2}'' \times 28''$, driving wheels 5' $1\frac{1}{2}''$ diameter, boiler pressure 213 lb per sq in, grate area 52 sq ft, axle loading $17\frac{1}{2}$ tons and tractive effort 41,492 lb. Their total weight in full working order is 165 tons.

With the exception of ten Central de Aragon-design Garratts, which were built in 1961, the 141Fs were Spain's final steam engines and one of the very last steam types to be built in Europe. Owing to modernisation, many have faced an untimely withdrawal, and make an ironic contrast with the numerous centurions for which Spain was so noted in the 1960s. Nevertheless, quite a number of 141Fs are still active and these 'pleasantly Spanish' engines will now fulfil the majority of the R.E.N.F.E.'s requirements for steam until its intended extinction in 1973 after which time one of the class will be put by for inclusion in the Spanish Railway Museum.

Ex-S.R. West Country/Merchant Navy Classes 4-6-2
Pl. 5, 34, 96

On the Sunday afternoon of 9 July, 1967, I sat in the hot sunshine on the grassy slopes of Upwey Bank, Weymouth, waiting to see the 14.07 Weymouth to Waterloo train depart; a train which signified not only the cessation of main-line express steam working in Britain, but also that of Bulleid's ex-Southern Railway Merchant Navy and West Country class Pacifics. For some time these engines, along with a few B.R. Standards, had constituted Britain's last links with main-line steam with their operation of the Waterloo–Salisbury, Southampton, Bournemouth and Weymouth services. As I waited, *Brentor,* a West Country, headed light down the bank on its last journey to Weymouth. For that weekend all the Southern Region's steam fleet, wherever they were, had to be despatched to either Nine Elms, Salisbury or Weymouth depots for withdrawal and subsequent despatch to breakers yards. The quietness of that secluded spot induced me to ponder over past adventures with these Pacifics, adventures which had begun the previous autumn when, in view of the drastic reduction in steam on my native London Midland Region, I resolved to journey to Southern England to savour the delights of these engines.

During that final year I covered most of the system, but autumn found me concentrating my activities in the New Forest between Southampton and Bournemouth filming the pacifics. Amid these beautiful surroundings blackberries abounded in the hedges whilst autumn had turned the forest into an auburn blaze. The Bulleid Pacifics' mournful whistles struck an idyllic harmony with the birds' low murmurings as train after train passed in this, steam's last blissful fling. The staccato bark of the B.R. standards was so different from the almost cultured raspings of the Pacifics, characterised by a leisurely stealth, whose soft pounding intensity stimulated one's senses. As autumn lengthened, the forest's moods changed and the flaming sunsets of evening gave way to a misty dampness in which the engine's exhausts would remain minutes after the train had passed. Rainy days added a mystique of their own and although gaps between trains were sometimes lengthy, one could enjoy nature at its best; wild flowers abounded by the linesides, whilst newts, lizards, snakes and toads became an everyday sight, in addition to many species of butterfly, some of which are peculiar to that area.

With the approach of winter I moved into Bournemouth where new photographic themes emerged, such as engines and people, engines on shed and engines by night, though quite a bit of photography was done on the 1 in 60 gradient which lies between Bournemouth and Poole – one of the legendary mariner ports of old England. However, those winter afternoons would usually find me on Bournemouth Central Station watching a Merchant Navy take the *Bourne-mouth Belle* on its 108-mile journey to Waterloo, and each day, a few minutes after 5 p.m., a Merchant Navy would draw in the spotless rake of Pullman coaches and an air of affluence would descend upon the station.

The arrival of spring brought an influx of diesels, and some of the best known Pacifics were withdrawn, while those that remained began to look increasingly unkempt. Further explorations westwards brought me to the towns of Wareham and Wool, through which the main line passed on its journey to the port and holiday town of Weymouth. Here then was this enthusiast's paradise, set in the twilight of Britain's steam age. With the warmer days of 1967, droves of enthusiasts from all over Britain descended onto the system where, despite a continual reduction in steam diagrams, combined with increasingly dirty engines, the majesty of steam prevailed—to the happiness and excitement of so many. Although preferring the line's more westerly parts, I recalled the long, pleasurable days at Worting Junction, the divergence point of the Bournemouth and Exeter lines, where the extra traffic created by Salisbury's engines coming off the Exeter line helped to offset the ever diminishing Bournemouth section.

It all had to end, and on the final Saturday when Merchant Navy *Holland Afrika Line* ran into Bournemouth with the 8.30 from Waterloo it was greeted by a vast crowd of people. By the afternoon Bournemouth shed was a hive of activity, hundreds of enthusiasts coming to pay their last respects as the surviving pacifics were despatched, light or in pairs, on their final runs to Weymouth. As West Country *Saunton* trundled out of the depot for the last time, all available engines saluted her. The gruff honking of the diesels, the lighter pitched B.R. Standards, and the clear tones of the S.R. Pacifics blended in an affray which could be heard all over Bournemouth. By night-time most engines had gone, for the depot was to close that weekend, and it was with acute sadness that evening that I witnessed the little farewell parties for the many staff for whom the end of the steam age meant redundancy from railway service.

Such were my reflections that afternoon as the sound of the mournful whistle of *Elder Dempster Lines* (*see* plate 96) reached my ears as it tackled the 1 in 51 climb before disappearing forever into the 1,360 yard long Wishing Well Tunnel. With plumes of white smoke rising up against the blue sky the Pacific, resplendent in her dark-green livery, lifted the train over the grades with such ease as to seemingly make a mockery of any plans for modernisation. With the diminishing sounds of *Elder Dempster* hammering through the tunnel, all that remained was the transitory wisp of smoke that oozed out of the tunnel mouth. It was all over, the morrow was for the diesel.

Perhaps the worst aspect of that final weekend was still to come, when, upon my arrival at Salisbury depot later that evening, I found it crammed full of engines, the majority of which had run down that day. All fires had been dropped, yet the engines were still in steam and through the evening silence which hung over the depot could be heard their hissings and gurglings, impregnating the air with that acrid aroma so peculiar to steam locomotives. Whenever before had so much power been put asunder? It was as if history were being haunted by its own ghosts. With reminiscences heavy on my mind I left that now macabre depot and continued my northward journey home.

Although the background history of these two classes has been copiously dealt with in other books I will describe it briefly here. The first Merchant Navy emerged from the Southern Railway's Eastleigh Works in 1941 as an air-smoothed express passenger engine capable of hauling 500-ton trains at speeds up to 70 m.p.h. Twenty-nine further engines were built and the class was put to work on the Southern's Dover, Bournemouth and Exeter lines. Considering the wartime conditions under which they were built, they possessed some very revolutionary features including all welded steel fireboxes with two thermic syphons, boxpok driving wheels for greater strength, special suspension arrangements, electric lighting throughout, and one of the best designed cabs ever to appear on a British steam engine – spacious, with all controls conveniently arranged to be easily accessible for the driver. Their most unusual feature, however, was the chain-driven valve-gear, all of which was enclosed in an oil-bath to reduce maintenance and wear. The locomotives were named to commemorate various shipping companies that had affinity with the Southern Railway at Southampton, and they quickly proved themselves to be excellent performers.

A lighter version, the 'West Countries', was prepared in 1945 and although having the same characteristics as the 'Merchant Navies', their axle loading was only 18¾ tons as opposed to 21 tons. This rendered them eminently suitable for use on secondary routes in the Southern's network, especially those lines west of Exeter. 110 examples were built between 1945 and 1950, the final ones being constructed by B.R. Named after towns in the west country, the engines carried beautiful scroll nameplates which incorporated the town's coat of arms, and others, known as the Battle of Britain series, commemorated squadrons and personalities that played an important part in World War II.

Despite their considerable success both classes had, by the mid-1950s, become far too unorthodox for the ever standardising British Railways, and accordingly they underwent a rebuilding which completely changed their appearance. This rebuilding included removal of the streamlined casing, reduction of the boiler pressure from 280 lb per sq in to 250 lb per sq in and conversion of the chain-driven valve-gear, to the traditional Walschaerts type. Not all of the lighter pacifics were rebuilt, a few surviving in their original condition until withdrawal from service. A comparison of both classes in rebuilt form may be drawn from the following specifications.

'Merchant Navy' Class: 3 cylinders 18″ × 24″, driving wheel diameter 6′ 2″, boiler pressure 250 lb per sq in, grate area $48\frac{1}{2}$ sq ft, tractive effort at 85 per cent of boiler pressure 33,495 lb, whilst the engine's weight in working order was 98 tons.

'West Country' Class: 3 cylinders $16\frac{3}{8}″$ × 24″, driving wheels 6′ 2″ diameter, boiler pressure 250 lb per sq in, grate area $38\frac{1}{4}$ sq ft, tractive effort at 85 per cent of boiler pressure 27,715 lb and the engine's weight in working order was 90 tons.

After their heroic finish, which included several unofficial 100 m.p.h. flings, the majority of the Southern Pacifics were quickly despatched to various South Wales scrapyards. Fortunately their fame ensured the preservation of both a rebuilt 'Merchant Navy' along with two unrebuilt light Pacifics. Quite a number of rust-covered examples still lie awaiting cutting up in Woodhams Scrapyard at Barry, and during the summer of 1971 came news of an attempt to retrieve *Bodmin,* a rebuilt 'West Country', with a view to restoring it in working order. If this plan achieves fruition it will fill an important gap in Britain's preserved locomotive stock.

D.B. 050 Class 2–10–0   Pl. 6, 8

The great distinction of these locomotives is that, quite apart from being an important type in the D.R.B.'s Locomotive Standardisation Plan, they formed the basis for the German war engines or 'Kriegslokomotiven', of which some 10,000 were built. This therefore made them the most numerous steam locomotive type in the world. As a class, the 50s may be regarded as the lighter sisters of the 44s, their 2 cylinders and 14.8 ton axle loading giving them a wide route availability for the operation of secondary mixed traffic services. The excellence of design, however, has caused them to be used on heavy main-line trains as well, and accordingly, they can be found today performing a very wide range of duties. It has often been said that much of the work entrusted to them is well beneath their capacity and undoubtedly this is true, but such lack of operational efficiency is counterbalanced by the widespread standardisation of design.

Initially the 50s were produced as successors to the ex-Prussian G10 0–10–0s (D.B. Class 057), and the first ones were built by Henschel in 1938. Over the next five years or so, a total in excess of 3,000 was constructed, many in foreign workshops during the German occupation. Large numbers of these 'foreign' engines remained in their country of origin and after the war 50s were taken into the locomotive stocks of Belgium, Denmark, France, Austria, Poland and Hungary. Some later 50s were built in simplified 'U.K.' form, and production of the 'Kriegsloks' 52 Class was by a further simplification of these 'U.K.' 50s (see page 128).

The 50s, which might be considered as a German equivalent of the British Black 5, are the D.B.'s most widely distributed and numerous type, with approximately 500 still in service. Ten engines, from the Köln Division, were subject to an experiment to discover whether they could be used effectively as shunting engines of lesser power. As a result the grate area was reduced, the superheated heating surface increased, and by means of a water chamber across the firebox a larger heating surface was created. In the power range of about 800 h.p., a fuel economy of seven per cent, combined with a 45°C higher steam temperature, was attained. During the 1950s thirty were equipped with Heinl Feed Water Heaters whilst others received Giesl Ejectors. In 1955 Henschel rebuilt a 50 with a Franco-Crosti pre-heater, thus creating a precedent for 30 members of the class. These engines, apart from one which was experimentally fitted for oil-burning, gave a seventeen per cent saving on coal consumption. None of these engines, however, remain in service today.

Leading dimensions are: 2 cylinders $23\frac{5}{8}'' \times 26''$, driving wheels $4' 7\frac{1}{8}''$ diameter, boiler pressure of 227 lb per sq in, grate area 42 sq ft, and a tractive effort of some 50,000 lb. Total length is 75' and the engines have a coal and water capacity of 8 tons and 5,730 gallons respectively.

Visitors to Germany are always intrigued by one of the 50s most noticeable characteristics – the fact that some of them possess a tender-cab. This idea, which originated in 1954, was developed by the Köln and Essen divisions as a result of a guards van shortage. Known as the 'Kabintender', it provides accommodation for guards and thus dispenses with the need for a separate van – because all German trains have continuous brakes, the traditional concept of a guards van no longer applies.

The D.B. authorities intend to dispense with steam traction by 1975 and it seems most likely that 50s will be the last engines to remain. In East Germany they are expected to survive longer, and out of the several hundred that remain in service there, a large number have recently been reboilered and fitted for oil-firing.

In the early part of this century the Prussian State Railways decided upon a standardisation scheme for their locomotives, and quite a number of the designs subsequently prepared, owing to the large numbers built, later formed an important backbone of 'Reichsbahn's' locomotive stock after Germany's railways came under state control in 1920. One of the principal types involved was the 2-cylinder P8 4–6–0 (later D.B. 038), a class that was destined to become one of the most prolific in the world. The effect that two world wars had upon their distribution and detail variations was considerable and they have since become a fascinating subject for the locomotive archivist.

The P8s were the first superheated 4–6–0s to appear, and it was the success of these superheated engines, combined with the incorporation of long travel valves, which convinced the Prussians that single expansion locomotives were adequate for their purposes. The design was the forerunner of the general utility 4–6–0s that were to become so popular in many countries and the P8s 17-ton axle loading gave them a wide route availability. Their use upon mixed traffic duties was widespread, notwithstanding the fact that the 'P' designation was a Prussian abbreviation for 'Personenzuglokomotiv' or 'secondary passenger engine'.

It was in 1906 that the first P8 was delivered from B.M.A.G. (Schwartzkopf) of Berlin and by 1924 some 3,000 were at work in Germany; a figure that had increased to 3,850 by the 1930s. Their boilers were interchangeable with the famous Prussian G10 0–10–0 freight engines (later D.B. 057 Class), and similar to the ones used by the Prussian T18 4–6–4Ts (later D.B. 078 Class). By 1930 no passenger locomotive type in the world was as numerically and territorially widespread as the P8. Some had been built for other German State Railways, whilst large numbers were constructed in Germany for service in Poland, Rumania, Lithuania, and France; in the latter case the M.I.D.I. Railway purchased 26 P8s at a price of 92,600 marks each. Of the leading German locomotive builders, Henschel had the greatest share in delivery and 792 engines originated from their Kassel works for service in Germany, whilst a further 52, fitted for oil-burning, were constructed for Rumania.

Further spreading of P8s occurred both during and immediately after both world wars because under armistice agreements, Germany was obliged to make reparations in the form of locomotives. After World War I batches were sent to France, Italy, Belgium and Greece, while the ending of the second great war saw P8s despatched to Luxembourg, Belgium, The Netherlands, Czechoslovakia and Russia.

Such a traumatic history inevitably rendered them as

subjects for innumerable detail variations and one of those that spring to mind is the fitting in the 1930s, of one with Caprotti valve gears and two with Lentz valve gears. Originally the class was built without smoke deflectors, but in 1925 they were given large D.R.B. ones, and from 1950 the smaller Witte ones of the present day were fitted by the D.B. This latter change also occurred on the East German D.R. Some members of the class were fitted for 'push and pull' working, despite the fact that it is rare to find a tender engine on such duties, but at one time they were seen in profusion, especially on suburban trains in the Frankfurt (Main) area. However, the most interesting experiment was the fascinating rebuilding undertaken by Krauss-Maffei whereupon two P8s were rebuilt as 4–6–4Ts and reclassified 78[10]. This took place after World War II when a shortage of suburban tank engines was causing the D.B. some concern; however, owing to the change to more modern forms of motive power, no further rebuilding took place and the two engines concerned were withdrawn in 1962.

During their latter days many received semi-elliptical, frameless tenders taken from scrapped 'Kriegslokomotive' of type 52 and while this did not necessarily improve the P8s' looks, it certainly heightened their character. Mercifully none of the D.B. engines ever received a Giesl ejector though in 1964 one was fitted experimentally to a D.R. P8. This spoilt the handsome outline but was justified economically by a substantial reduction in coal consumption. This has resulted in Giesl ejectors being fitted to 45 of the D.R.'s P8s out of their present-day total of 130.

The leading dimensions of the class are: 2 cylinders $22\frac{1}{8}''$ × $24\frac{1}{8}''$, driving wheel diameter 5' $8\frac{5}{8}''$, boiler pressure 171 lb per sq in, grate area 28.4 sq ft, whilst the total weight of engine in working order is 77 tons.

Originally the D.B. intended to replace their P8s with the 023 2–6–2s, which were introduced in 1950 for mixed-traffic duties, but owing to a curtailment of all steam building, because of modernisation plans, only 105 023s were constructed, and as a result of this the D.B. still possessed several hundred P8s as recently as the early 1960s. However, since that time withdrawals have been heavy and it is felt that 1972 will be the final year for them on the D.B. Only a handful remain and these are confined to the Stuttgart Region, in common with their ex-Prussian relations the T18 4–6–4Ts, where they work secondary passenger services, along with an occasional freight, in the Black Forest area.

In Western Germany the towns of Rottweil, Tübingen, and Horb have become host to the surviving remnants of this once great class and to be in this delightful area seeing them at work is a fine experience, as one so readily assimilates

125

their fascinating history and vintage – *objets d'art* indeed!

So many times over recent years we have had to bid farewell to distinctive locomotive designs, but parting with the P8s will be none the easier for that, and many locomotive students have made the pilgrimage to the Black Forest area to see them in action. Some compensation may be gleaned from the fact that many are still at work in East Germany, and other survivors can be found in Romania and Poland; in the latter country the large smoke deflectors situated on the running plates dramatically alter their appearance. However, in these countries the political situation has rendered the P8s considerably less accessible than their West German counterparts. Three have been preserved, one in Belgium and two in West Germany.

C.P. Metre Gauge Kessler 2–6–0T Nos E81–86/E111–114
Pl. 9, 26, 73

The 2–6–0T arrangement is widely used on Portugal's metre-gauge railways and three different designs totalling some 20 engines are in operation; in fact these constitute almost one third of the entire metre-gauge stock. Of these 2–6–0s the most magnificent is this batch of six engines, which were built by Emil Kessler for the C.N. in 1886, and nowadays numbered E81–6. They are the oldest locomotives in Portugal. Quite apart from age, their archaic looks render them akin to something from an Emmett cartoon; I do not say this disparagingly, but they have every possible ingredient one could wish for in a humorously-construed vintage steam engine: massive chimneys which completely dwarf their small smoke-boxes, two huge ornately-shaped domes, elongated front end, outside cylinders with Allen Link Motion, square cabs and an immense toolbox and jack placed in front of the side tanks. The overall effect is elongated and slightly hideous. However, unlike the engine illustrated, some members of the class possess elegant copper-capped chimneys – a feature that Emmett would certainly have insisted upon. When seeing these 85-year-old engines for the first time I found it hard to believe that such gems could exist in the 1970s and although, for many people, the pinnacle of C.P. metre-gauge engines is reached with the famous Mallet Tanks, my choice would be these 2–6–0Ts which never fail to hold me awestruck.

All six still survive and are well distributed: Nos E81/2 are based at Tua for working the Bragança Line, Nos E83/5/6 are at Boa Vista and E84 belongs to Sernada do Vouga. They are almost identical to a later series of Kessler 2–6–0Ts, numbered E111–114, the first pair of which were built in 1904 and the latter two in 1908, again to the C.N.'s requirements. In this series Nos E111–3 are assigned to Tua and No

114 to Boa Vista. The dimensions of both classes are 2 cylinders $13\frac{3}{4}'' \times 19\frac{1}{2}''$, driving wheels $3' 3\frac{1}{2}''$ diameter, boiler pressure 142 lb per sq in, and a grate area of 12 sq ft. Their length over buffers is 31' and they weigh 32 tons.

What old world magic these engines conjure up; to see them on the Porto complex is memorable. Once past Senhora da Hora the lines pass through soft, wooded landscape with decorative wayside stations abounding every few miles. These stations are beautifully kept with arrays of gorgeous flowers and show a pride of environment which has long since passed in many European countries. Over such lines these little Kessler tanks puff along, like an adventure story come true, their resplendency further confirming the pride which exists, not only for Portugal's locomotives, but also for the railway itself.

S.N.C.F. 140C Class 2–8–0 Pl. 10

First introduced in 1913 by the Etat Railway, this class of 2-cylinder, 2–8–0 heavy freight engine was an integral part of French motive power for some 50 years. The overall soundness of design, combined with an axle load of only 16 tons, rendered them as an ideal standard type and, following the outbreak of the First World War, many were built to the order of the French Government for operating heavy wartime traffic.

Building of the engines commissioned for wartime use commenced in 1916. Many were constructed in France by the Artilleries Lourdes Voies Ferrées (A.L.V.F.), but a considerable number were also built in Great Britain both by the North British Locomotive Company of Glasgow and the Nasmyth Wilson Company of Manchester. Construction continued until 1920, by which time 370 examples were in existence. Over the following years the class became widespread in France and until recently they remained one of the last surviving remnants of French steam design. Of the handful that survived, the majority were centred around Verdun, a sub-depot of Chalons-sur-Marne, in the Est region.

The duty of the Verdun engines was to operate stone trains between Dugny and Conflans, and in so doing they became a principal attraction for locomotive students from all over Europe. A four-mile climb out of Verdun had to be negotiated by the loaded trains and frequently two 140Cs were used double-headed. In a country like France, whose railways are now almost entirely modernised, it was refreshing to find such veterans still at work, albeit in a remote part of the country, and the friendliness and pride radiated by the engine crews provided a perfect foil for what was one of the most exciting steam-worked lines in Europe.

However, 140Cs may still be found on the route from

127

Gray to Troyes. This line, which also has a branch off to Chaumont, is part of a separate system known as the C.F.T.A.: Compagnie Generale des Chemins de Fer et des Transports Automobiles. The company operates several secondary routes using locomotives on hire from the S.N.C.F. and apart from the 140Cs, which are based at Gray, a few other vintage French designs may also be found within the C.F.T.A. ranks. This however is unlikely to continue for much longer, since closure of the entire system has recently been advocated.

The leading dimensions are: cylinders $23\frac{1}{4}'' \times 25\frac{3}{8}''$, driving wheels 4' $8\frac{3}{8}''$ diameter, boiler pressure 171 lb per sq in, and a grate area of 34 sq ft. The total weight in working order is 118 tons, of which the engine constitutes 73 tons, whilst the coal and water capacities are 5 tons and 4,000 gallons respectively. Such weights are certainly far from excessive in proportion to the dimensions and power developed, which at 75 per cent of the normal pressure, is 31,140 lb. All locomotives in this class are superheated and many have been fitted with either A.C.F.I. or Daebeg feed-water heaters. One of the North British built engines is set by for preservation in the railway museum at Mulhouse.

Ö.B.B. 52 Class 2–10–0   Pl. 11

Upon the commencement of World War II, the German State Railway's freight locomotive stock needed to be greatly augmented. As a result the standard 44, 50 2–10–0 classes were increased to immense proportions both in Germany and, as the war progressed, in the workshops of occupied countries. However, from 1942, shortage of both materials and skilled workers called for economisations and simplifications. Accordingly, a plan was drawn up to build war engines in two stages: intermediate and final. The former were known as Ubergangskriegslokomotive, or U.K., which were simplified versions of classes 44, 50, while implementation of the final stage created the famous 'Kriegsloks', class 52, which were an even more drastic simplification of the U.K. 50 Class.

In mass producing the 52s, a tremendous saving in labour was achieved because they were almost entirely welded in construction. The 'Austerity' simplifications included removal of all superfluous parts such as large smoke deflectors, feed domes, feed-water heater systems, cylinder relief valves, and all other parts were worked on only as far as necessary for their efficient operation. Other features were the incorporation of welded steel fire-boxes and frames, which were developed partly as bar frames, but mainly as welded plate frames. A very simple type of bogie tender was used in which a semi-circular water tank was incorporated, so dispensing

128

with a need for the conventional tender under frame.

With the intensification of hostilities, these engines spread in thousands across war-torn Europe and one of their major uses was to assist the Germans in their attempted conquest of Russia. Upon the failure of this campaign many 52s were captured by the Russians and converted to their 5′ 0″ gauge. It is rumoured that some of these engines are still in service today.

Having overrun much of Europe, the Germans found a great deal of track suitable for locomotives possessing an 18-ton axle load and they found themselves in the position of having a 19½-ton axle engine in their Class 44, which was too heavy, and two 15-ton types in Classes 50, 52, which were not as powerful as the track could bear. Therefore, a heavier version of the 52 class was prepared, with an axle load of 17¼ tons. Designated Class 42, these engines possessed a 52-type chassis but had larger cylinders and a boiler, identical to the 44 Class except for a shorter barrel. Over 800 42s were built, though these diminish in importance when compared alongside the 52s, of which 6,300 were built.

It was inevitable that upon the ending of hostilities there would be a surplus of 'Kriegsloks', and many were given as war reparations. It was said that at one time they could be seen at work in almost every standard-gauge European country. Some survived on the D.B. until the early 1960s, after which they rather remarkably disappeared, despite the fact that a few were constructed for West Germany in post-war years! However, a reminder of them remained in West Germany in the form of their semi-elliptical tenders, many of which were taken over by ex-Prussian P8 4–6–0s.

Fortunately, some 700 'Kriegsloks' remain on today's D.R. where, in common with post-war D.B. engines, they have received smoke-deflectors. The D.R. have rebuilt many of their 50/52s with new standard boilers and some of the 52s have Giesl Ejectors, whilst 28 are fitted with powdered coal-firing apparatus. Their sister class, the 42s, have also disappeared from the D.B., the last ones surviving in the Saar Valley until 1962, and those that passed to the D.R. have also become extinct.

Plate number 11 illustrates two Ö.B.B. Austrian Federal Railway 52s, because both during and immediately after the German occupation many 'Kriegsloks' were built in Austria by Vienna Locomotive Works, Floridsdorf. When Austria's railways regained their former identity, many of these engines were absorbed into Ö.B.B. stock, and the Austrians further differentiated their 52s' classification by designating those with bar frames as Class 152. Approximately 100 still remain active in Austria and as such constitute the most numerous steam type to be found in that country. Apart from their widespread use on freight workings, the Ö.B.B. also employ them on a range of passenger duties.

Principal dimensions of the 'Kriegsloks' are: 2 cylinders $23\frac{5}{8}'' \times 26''$, driving wheels 4' $7\frac{1}{8}''$ diameter, boiler pressure 227 lb per sq in, and grate area 42 sq ft. The total weight of the engines in working order is 84 tons.

Even the most liberally-minded locomotive connoisseur could hardly regard the 52s as handsome; indeed it would be difficult to imagine a more austere design. I can never dissociate them from war, and one can so easily picture how perfectly they blended with the terrible time for which they were created. Few engines conjure up such a poignant atmosphere and to the imagination they whisper tales of war. In Austria, further starkness is added to them by fitting Giesl ejectors to the majority of the class, although the two engines illustrated possess their original D.R.-type chimneys.

Without doubt, the 'Kriegsloks' are one of history's most fascinating locomotive types and it is fortunate that many are still active, albeit principally behind the Iron Curtain. Apart from countries already mentioned, survivors may still be found at work in Poland, Romania, Czechoslovakia, Turkey, Jugoslavia, Hungary and Bulgaria. Furthermore, they could, until very recently, be seen in Norway where one is to be preserved at Hamar.

R.E.N.F.E. 241F Class 4–8–2   Pl. 12

Massive steam engines have always evoked feelings of awe; they are essentially different. Certainly they lack the quaintness associated with many smaller engines but the culmination of majesty and power radiated by them more than compensates for this. In these closing years of steam it is heartening to think that some giants still exist, though even in days of steam supremacy 4–8–2s were not a common type. Certainly the world has known many bigger engines, especially in America, but in European traditions 4–8–2s and 4–8–4s (see page 141) possess a unique aura of their own and it is only in Spain that the two types can be found working side by side.

The story of 4–8–2s in Spain began, rather surprisingly perhaps, as long ago as 1925 when satisfaction with the 4–8–0 type led the N.O.R.T.E. to order sixty-six 4-cylinder de Glehn system compound 4–8–2s for mixed-traffic work. These engines came out only a few weeks after the first European 4–8–2s had appeared in France. In the same year the M.Z.A. entered the 4–8–2 field with an enlarged version of their 1400 Class 4–8–0 (page 159) and these were followed in 1939 by their ten famous semi-streamlined 4–8–2s from Maquinista. Exactly why the M.Z.A. decided to introduce streamlined engines is a mystery. I can hardly imagine that it was for speed, as Spanish trains were never particularly fast; it has been suggested that they were merely following the current trend and without doubt these engines bore some superficial resemblance to Gresley's L.N.E.R. A4s. The same year saw the N.O.R.T.E. rebuild one of their 1925 engines on the principle adopted by M. Andre Chapelon with the P.O. Pacifics in France. This involved the redesigning of cylinders and valves, the incorporation of Daebeg O.C. Poppet Valves along with the fitting of a double Kylchap blast-pipe. After nationalisation, the R.E.N.F.E. continued this modified type with twenty-eight new engines between 1946 and 1948.

The largest and final 4–8–2 development in Spain came with the locomotive illustrated, which was one of a R.E.N.F.E. standard class numbering fifty-seven engines, all of which were built by Maquinista between 1944 and 1952. Initially they were built to operate the heavily-graded ex-M.Z.A. lines from Madrid to Alicante and Seville. The class has 2 cylinders with O.C. Lentz Valves along with Kylchap double-blast pipes and chimneys. All locomotives were fitted to burn oil as it would have been impossible to handfire their 57 sq ft of grate area, especially with the low quality, soft coal available to Spanish engines. Their boilers were interchangeable with those of the R.E.N.F.E.'s massive 2–10–2 Santa Fé mentioned on page 134, and similar to the R.E.N.F.E. 4–8–4s (page 141). The leading dimensions are 2 cylinders $25\frac{3}{16}'' \times 28''$, driving wheels $5' 8\frac{7}{8}''$ diameter, boiler pressure 227 lb per sq in, axle loading $20\frac{1}{2}$ tons and their total weight in full working order is 201 tons. All engines are fitted with A.C.F.I. feed-water heaters and T.I.A. water treatment is also incorporated.

When talking of T.I.A. water treatment, it is interesting to note that water in many parts of Spain is highly unsuitable for locomotives and, if used in an untreated state, leaves vast deposits of scale in the boilers and fire-boxes. These deposits not only militate against the locomotives' steaming capacity but also lessen considerably the life of tubes, tube plates and stays and, as amazing as it may seem, it was not uncommon to remove a ton of scale from the larger locomotives' boilers during overhaul. The T.I.A. water purifiers now fitted into the locomotive tenders have overcome this problem and additionally have saved vast sums of money in de-scaling and corrosion costs.

Modernisations on the R.E.N.F.E. have rendered many of these 4–8–2s surplus to requirements and quite a number have been withdrawn, despite the fact that they are a comparatively modern type. The survivors are now principally working the ex-N.O.R.T.E. lines around Miranda and may be seen at such places as Alsasua and Pamplona. Late in 1970, several withdrawn members of the class were over- 131 hauled and returned to traffic during a motive power shortage and at the time of writing these engines are still active. My last recollection of them was on a rainy afternoon at Alsasua in the early spring of 1971 when one piloted a 141F on a Pamplona-bound freight train – what a sight they made as they pulled away from the yards which were set against a backdrop of snowy mountain peaks! With exhausts rising high and steam leaking from every gland they headed eastward, the 241F completely dwarfing the smaller engine. Enthusiastically we took up the chase by road intrepidly following their exhaust trails but they showed us a clean pair of heels and after some miles we gave up and spiritlessly returned to Alsasua.

Very isolated examples of the N.O.R.T.E. 4–8–2s still work between Salamanca and Medina whilst others lie derelict at Alsasua. All the M.Z.A. 4–8–2s are now withdrawn and, in the case of the streamliners, all ten stand in a single line at Burgos.

C.P. Metre Gauge 2–4–6–0T Mallet Nos E181–182/E201-216 Pl. 14, 30, 20, 48, 81

These stately engines are the manifestation of the Mallet type in Portugal and are the only engines of their kind in Europe. The Minho and Douro division of Portugal's State Railway obtained sixteen examples between 1911 and 1923: Nos 201/4 in 1911, Nos 205/6 in 1913 and the final ten Nos 207/216 in 1923. Furthermore in 1923, two additional engines Nos E181/2 were built for the North of Portugal Railway. In common with the smaller 0–4–4–0T Mallets page 139, all were built by Henschel of Germany as 4-cylinder compounds, and these two types combined constitute little short of half Portugal's active metre-gauge steam stock. These 2–4–6–0T Mallets have their leading set of driving wheels driven by the two low-pressure cylinders, the whole assembly being mounted on an articulating bissel-truck, while the six rear axles which are attached to the main frame are activated by the high-pressure cylinders. This articulation enables such large engines as these to operate over difficult lines like the Corgo and Sabor tributaries of the Douro Valley, for they possess sufficient power to tackle the many adverse gradients, often with very heavy trains. Their ability to negotiate sharp curves of up to 65-yard radius is another factor in their long success story. They are the largest, though not the most powerful, C.P. metre-gauge engines and the class is characterised by the following dimensions: 4 outside cylinders H.P. (2) $13\frac{3}{4}'' \times 21\frac{1}{2}''$, L.P. (2) $19\frac{1}{2}'' \times 21\frac{1}{2}''$, driving wheels 3' $7\frac{1}{4}''$ diameter, boiler pressure 199 lb per sq in, grate area 22 sq ft and a tractive effort at 75 per cent boiler pressure of 19,030 lb. The total weight is 60 tons and length over buffers 40'.

All eighteen engines are still in active service: the two ex-N.P. examples along with five ex-M.D. ones belong to Sernada and may be seen between Viseu and Espinho, whereas the remainder are divided between the Douro Valley towns of Régua and Pocinho for working the 61-mile Corgo line and 66-mile Sabor line respectively. Over these latter two routes they have almost a complete monopoly of steam operation. The two types are almost identical in appearance except that the ex-N.P. examples have only one side window in the cab, whereas the ex-M.D. engines possess two. All, however, are well endowed with brasswork and by any standards are extremely fine-looking engines. Their mastery of operation is further emphasised by the remarkable quietness of their exhausts.

I always associate these engines with the vine-clad Corgo Valley for this is undoubtedly the best place to see them. Seven are assigned to this route and the plates show them at work with the mixed trains which, although principally comprised of freight vans, always carry at least a couple of ancient, 4-wheel passenger coaches in which the local populace travel to market or town. At grape harvest the quiet daily routine of the Corgo line suddenly becomes transformed and life acquires an uncharacteristic bustle. This is a time when the trains are packed to the roof with grape pickers, many having travelled in from miles around. The Mallets haul these loaded trains up the valley, with sounds of music bursting from every coach: accordians, guitars, mouth organs and drums combining in an affray which can be heard way through the valley, for the harvesters make much merriment before the serious business of grape-picking begins. Upon the harvest's completion villages all over the hills resound with noisy festivals, which carry on late into the warm Portuguese nights. In this delightful world these 2-4-6-0T Mallets are inextricably bound.

One of the class working from Pocinho, No. E209, is fitted with a Giesl ejector; what the economical effects of this are I have no idea, but aesthetically it borders on sacrilege, and one pines for the replacement of the slender copper-capped chimney which does so much for the distinctive air of these engines (*see* plate no. 14). Certainly it appears that the C.P. have no intention of continuing this practice, and fortunately so, as the thought of these lovely locomotives being disfigured by the uncouthness of a Giesl ejector is akin to something out of a nightmare.

P.V. 2-6-2T, 2-6-0   **Pl. 16, 17, 82, 83**

One of the most enthralling aspects of railway enthusiasm is the ramification of the subject into specialised sections. This is clearly a fascinating topic in itself, and a treatise might one day be written on it, but one of the most interesting factors is that of the difference between the 'broad' and 'narrow' gauges. Although the term 'narrow gauge' is arbitrary, it usually refers to lines whose width is less than 4' $8\frac{1}{2}''$ and it is these small lines that attract an immense amount of attention.

The unique attraction of narrow-gauge railways is difficult to define, but often they are rustic and somewhat antiquated systems and by their very quaintness one feels a strong sense of endearment towards them. Whether operating as preserved lines or commercial ones, the European narrow-gauge railways are somewhat poverty stricken and are noted for their ancient locomotives and rolling stock.

Until recently Spain was a paradise for narrow gauge lovers and it was estimated in the early 1950s that over 50 steam-worked lines were to be found throughout the country ranging from 4' $8\frac{1}{2}''$ down to 600 mm. The changing face of Spain over the last two decades has rendered many of these defunct while a number of those that remain have been electrified, but one important system that is still almost 100 per cent steam-worked is that of the Compania Minero Siderurgica de Ponferrada or better known as the Ponferrada – Villablino Railway (P.V.).

Situated in the north-western part of Spain some 80 miles west of Leon on the R.E.N.F.E. line to Vigo, Ponferrada constitutes a city of some importance and it is from there that the 40-mile, metre-gauge line wends its way northwards to Villablino. Ponferrada is the southern terminus of the line and it is there that the main depot, workshops and exchange sidings with the R.E.N.F.E. are situated. The purpose of the line is to carry coal from the mines in the Villablino area down to the R.E.N.F.E. at Ponferrada and in the course of so doing it additionally serves power stations and briquetting works. One of the most fascinating points about the system is that it is fed by a number of 600 mm lines, some of which are steam-worked by diminutive 0–4–0Ts.

I must state at this point that in no way is the P.V. a rustic concern for although it is truly in the best of narrow-gauge traditions it is a well maintained and highly efficient railway, and furthermore returns a handsome profit. The line carries 2 million tons of coal per year, much of which is conveyed in modern steel hopper waggons, and it was for this traffic that the R.E.N.F.E. originally built the massive Sante Fé 2–10–2s in 1942 which, prior to electrification, operated between Ponferrada and the Atlantic seaport of La Coruna. In addition to the mineral traffic, the P.V. also operates a passenger service and although this only consists of two return trains per day it is very well used and provides an important local service.

The P.V. route is single track, but owing to the traffic density it has many passing points and is covered throughout by two-aspect, colour-light signalling. For much of the journey the line follows the course of the River Sil, and at the Villablino end the scenery becomes very dramatic. Some ambitious engineering works have been constructed as a result of the River being dammed for hydro-electric power. Most noteworthy amongst these are viaducts over reservoirs and a long tunnel upon the approach to Villablino. It has been suggested that eventually the entire line will be converted to 5′ 6″ gauge and possibly electrified. On the line itself there is considerable evidence to support this, not least of which is the greater loading gauge of the recently constructed tunnels. Should this transition be executed, it would obviously take some time and thus it would be a reasonable supposition that steam power might remain for some years yet.

The motive power is both varied and impressive although nothing older than 1913 may be found on the metre-gauge metals. Basically there are two types: a batch of ten 2–6–2Ts, and a batch of ten 2–6–0s. The 2–6–2Ts of which No. 7 (Plate 17) is an example were all built by Baldwin in 1919; they are maintained in a magnificent black livery with red wheels and white rims. All are named, with brass nameplates situated on the cabside. These handsome engines are of classic American design and even have brass bells mounted on their boilers; unfortunately these are not rung, but nevertheless they make a fine adornment.

A controversy has occurred in deciding the precise designation of the 2–6–0s, for their short 4-wheel tenders are actually mounted on the locomotives' main frames which, in theory, should render them a tank type. However they are ostensibly a tender design and they are generally known as such, conforming as they do to a type of Engerth locomotive. The P.V.'s oldest Engerth was built by Maffei in 1913 and five by Krauss followed in 1920 (see plate nos 82/83). All were obtained second-hand by the P.V. In 1950 two further examples were built by Macosa of Spain followed by the final two in 1956; these four engines were delivered new to the P.V. Plate no. 16 shows one of the 1956 Engerths, which are a modified and larger version of the original design and as such represent the ultimate in present-day P.V. power. Apart from the 600-mm gauge engines, the P.V. company possesses other miscellaneous types including some vintage 5′ 6″-gauge locomotives used for shunting the coal screens and exchange sidings at Ponferrada. Thus it may be seen that the company operates steam locomotives of three different gauges.

The locomotive variety, high-traffic density and beautiful

terrain make the P.V. one of the most attractive systems in Europe and one that is increasingly being put onto enthusiasts' itinerary lists. Long may it remain, for to find so prolific a system, almost 100 per cent steam-operated, in the 1970s is something not to be missed and despite the efficiency with which it is worked it still possesses plenty of that 'narrow-gauge charm'.

Hunslet 'Austerity' 0–6–0ST   Pl. 19, 31, 33, 39, 40, 41, 78

Today, steam in Britain is becoming increasingly difficult to find. It is, apart from preserved lines, entirely confined to industrial use, and its decline in this environment over the last five years has surprised even the most pessimistic enthusiasts. Much of what does remain is in the hands of one of Britain's great 'stalwart' designs – the Hunslet 'Austerity' 0–6–0ST. These engines will go down in history with such distinguished types as Ramsbottom's 0–6–0s of the L.N.W.R., the 5700 Class Pannier Tanks of the G.W.R. and the Stanier Black 5s of the L.M.S.R., along with a number of other important British classes. No less than 484 Austerities were built and their story in terms of building origins, distribution, variations and experimental modifications is one of the most fascinating in locomotive history.

Ever since 1872 Hunslet have been important British locomotive builders; they have manufactured engines for countries all over the world in addition to supplying the needs of a very diverse home market. For almost fifty years Hunslet have become noted for their 0–6–0ST designs; types that have widely permeated British industry. The forerunner of these designs might be regarded as the 16″ Saddle Tanks of 1923 (see page 176). In 1937 Guest, Keen and Baldwin's Iron and Steel Co. requested a more powerful type than these 16″ engines, which they were using at that time, and accordingly Hunslet produced their 48150 Class of 0–6–0STs with 18″ cylinders. Nine of these were built up to 1942, by which time Hunslet's improved 50550 Class, with enlarged saddle tanks, had appeared (see pages 180–81).

During these years, Britain was in the throes of World War II and it was realised that the success of forthcoming military operations in Europe, following the secretly planned invasion of France, would rely upon efficient transport arrangements for many thousands of tons of supplies. Locomotive production, which until this time had been restricted, became a priority item and it was vitally necessary to select the most suitable types for the jobs in hand. At the resulting Ministry of Supply conference it was decreed that for heavy shunting, an engine capable of starting 1,100-ton trains on level track, 550-ton trains on inclines of 1 in 100 and 300-ton trains on inclines of 1 in 50, was necessary, and the honour fell to Hunslet for a locomotive based on their 50550 Class. The 'Austerities', as the new engines were called, differed outwardly from the 50550s only in cab and bunker outlines, the latter being designed to give a 5-cwt increase in coal-carrying capacity.

The Austerities' principal dimensions are: 2 inside cylinders 18″ × 26″, driving wheels 4′ 3″ diameter, boiler pressure 170 lb per sq in, tractive effort 23,870 lb and a grate area of 16.8 sq ft. Their maximum axle load is $16\frac{1}{2}$ tons, and total weight in working order 48 tons. The coal and water capacities are $2\frac{1}{4}$ tons and 1,200 gallons respectively.

On 1 January, 1943 the first Austerity was steamed at Hunslet's Leeds works, a further 149 following over a period of 3 years. Not all of these came from Hunslet, as other manufacturers, namely Andrew Barclay, W. G. Bagnall, Hudswell Clarke, Robert Stephenson and Hawthorn, Vulcan Foundry and the Yorkshire Engine Co., were commissioned to build them, although in the latter company's case the engines were not destined to appear until 1954. The War Department loaned some to the L.M.S.R., whilst others went to the Ministry of Fuel and Power, and before long they became established in Army depots and Governmental establishments throughout the length and breadth of Britain.

The cessation of hostilities in 1945 found Austerities scattered far and wide across Europe, for many were surplus to War Department requirements, and they were therefore put up for sale. Twenty-seven were loaned to the Dutch State Railway, who subsequently purchased them in 1947, and some went to the Dutch State Mines. Others were sold to industrial and light railways in France and six remained in North Africa. Many were stored abroad for a time, and not all returned to Britain—the fate of these engines will probably never be known. In 1946 the L.N.E.R. purchased 75 Austerities, which became their celebrated J94 Class. Sales continued throughout British industry, the largest quantity going to the National Coal Board, who adopted them as standard shunters at collieries in England, Scotland and Wales, and indeed they continued to order new batches until 1964, despite a decision in some areas to replace steam with diesels. The War Department retained 90 for their own use in British depots, surprisingly enough, ordering 14 new examples in 1952. During the spread of these engines throughout British industry, they became subject to innumerable variations, their liveries diversified considerably, and many acquired names, some especially suitable such as *Hurricane, Warrior, Revenge* and *Warspite,* bestowed by the N.W. division of the N.C.B.

A considerable reduction in coal consumption has been effected by fitting many with Giesl ejectors, whereas others incorporate Hunslet's Special Blast Pipe; a device fitted in order to comply with local authorities' Clean Air Act which is a serious antagonism to industrial steam's future! Designed by Hunslet, this blast pipe necessitates major modifications to overcome the problem of emitting black smoke. The first of these rebuilds was done by Hunslet in 1961 and quite a number have since been so treated by the N.C.B. Further sophistications applied to certain engines are the fitting of electric lighting, incorporation of 'walkie-talkie' radios, and a few with mechanical stokers, including one which aspired to the heights of having a diesel engine concealed in its bunker to actuate the mechanical stoker! Countless detail variations occur, such as engines with flangeless centre drivers. These and similar diversifications provide an endless source of interest when one visits the various systems upon which these engines are still at work.

The Austerities' history might one day be written in its entirety, but meanwhile suffice it to say that these classic British engines are undeserving of the disdain bestowed upon them by British enthusiasts. It has for some years been fashionable to condemn any Austerity design, but let it be remembered that apart from these engines' magnificent performances, they have done much to extend the life of steam power. I estimate that over 100 are still in operation in Britain, principally on the N.C.B. and perhaps the best places to see them are on the South Wales coalfields, the Castleford area collieries in Yorkshire and the Cumberland coalfield. Already five have been preserved, including two from the Longmoor Military Railway, which are now at Rolvenden, headquarters of the Kent and East Sussex Railway.

My colour plates relating to these engines depict them at work in and around Whitehaven. Whitehaven's collieries are situated on the cliff-tops and coal lifted from Haig Colliery is Austerity-hauled along the cliffs to Ladysmith for washing, after which it is returned to Haig for transfer down a rope incline into Whitehaven Docks, either for export by sea to the Isle of Man or Ireland, or onto the connection with B.R. for conveyance to Workington Iron and Steel Works.

In the early summer of 1971, I was privileged to a night journey between Haig and Ladysmith on *Stanley,* a Giesl-fitted Austerity. It seemed almost incomprehensible that in 1971 such a thrilling journey could be undertaken in Britain. A full moon lit the sea as our Austerity forged its way along with a heavy coal train. The rhythms of steam leaking from the glands combined tantalisingly with *Stanley*'s exhaust beats, whilst an incessant shower of sparks emitted from the chimney bit like tracer into the night sky. Amid fire and steam we forged on, propelling our coal waggons through the blackness. To anyone watching our passage it might have been just some old colliery engine, but in truth it was one of steam's majestic rearguards, the triumphant and all-conquering Hunslet Austerity.

C.P. Metre Gauge 0–4–4–0T Mallet Nos E151–152/E161–170
Pl. 22, 37, 55, 69, 70, 89

Perhaps Portugal's most noted steam engines are the two series of Henschel-built Mallet Tanks of which these engines are the smaller. They are 4-cylinder compound machines with the two low-pressure cylinders placed in front and these, along with the first two coupled axles, are mounted on an articulated Bissel Truck. The high-pressure cylinders to the rear drive the fixed axles, this assembly being attached to the main frames. The Mallet principle is ideal on routes which contain many gradients, curves and bridges, as the articulation enables large and powerful locomotives to traverse the curves, whilst the two sets of driving wheels give the advantage of a light-axle loading with maximum adhesion. The size of these engines may be seen from their dimensions of 4 outside cylinders 2 H.P. $12\frac{1}{2}'' \times 21\frac{1}{2}''$, 2 L.P. $18\frac{3}{4}'' \times 21\frac{1}{2}''$, driving wheels 3' $7\frac{1}{4}''$ diameter, boiler pressure 171 lb per sq in and a grate area of 15 sq ft.

The first two Nos 151/2 were built in 1905 for the North of Portugal Railway while the remaining ten were Minho and Douro engines which came in two batches, Nos E161/4 in 1905, followed in 1908 by Nos E165/70. Of the two ex-N.P. engines one is now out of use, lying derelict at Lousado, and the other sees occasional use as the Tâmega line's only steam engine. Notwithstanding this all ten ex-M.D. engines are very much on the active list, being based at Porto (Boa Vista) depot for working the intensive service out of Trindade. Boa Vista is situated alongside Avenida da França station between Trindade and Senhora da Hora; it was the original metre-gauge terminus in Porto but was considered to be too far from the city centre, and accordingly the line was extended through some rather adventurously-built cuttings and tunnels to the present day terminus at Trindade (see plate no. 9).

The Porto metre-gauge complex is comprised of a circular system some 94 miles round, embracing Trindade with Senhora da Hora, Póvoa de Varzim, Famalicão, Lousado, Guimarães, Fafe and Trofa. Over this network these 0–4–4–0T Mallets are by far the most prolific type (see map page 160). The route from Trindade to Senhora da Hora is of special interest as it is double-track metre-gauge main line; over this section the rush hours bring excitingly dense traffic. After parting company at Senhora with the Póvoa route, the Fafe line passes through agricultural and wooded countryside until it reaches Trofa whereupon it joins the 5' 6" Minho line from Porto. Thence it runs northwards to Lousado and Familicão over a mixed-track single line, the metre-gauge metals fitting neatly between the 5' 6" ones. This must be one of Europe's most incredible steam-worked sections for each day it provides the unbelievable spectacle of a 1905 metre gauge 0-4-4-0T Mallet being followed minutes later, ostensibly over the same metals, by a 50-year-old 5' 6"-gauge, 4-cylinder compound Pacific. Although traffic over this mixed section is far from heavy one could never be disappointed with such fascinating operations. At Lousado the Fafe line diverges eastwards whilst at Famalicão, which is at the end of the mixed-gauge section, the metre-gauge line swings away westwards to Póvoa and thus completes the circle back to Trindade. A platformed spur is placed at the north end of Lousado station to enable trains from Fafe to continue northwards without reversing.

At one time this network was controlled by two separate concerns: the Porto, Póvoa and Famalicão Railway Co. and the Guimarães Railway Co., the latter operating between Trofa and Fafe and forming a system with only one link to Porto. After the incorporation of these entities into the North of Portugal Railway in 1928, the line from Trofa to Senhora was built, and this formed a circular and completely unified network. Time spent on these lines is truly rewarding, the towns ranging from Póvoa with its open Atlantic aspect to Guimarães with its castles and cathedrals, while on the locomotive side, quite apart from the array of broad-gauge engines over the mixed section, one can enjoy a selection of machines ranging from 2-6-0Ts of 1886 to 2-8-2Ts of 1931, not forgetting of course the ubiquitous 0-4-4-0T Mallets.

Rush hours at Trindade are equally enthralling with steam-hauled trains either arriving or departing every fifteen minutes or so. The quaint engines look almost ridiculous against the modern office blocks which tower high above the station. Here the city's commuter fraternity comes on weekday mornings and a Mallet rumbles out of the tunnel pulling its rattling string of ancient four-wheeled coaches, and with billowing brown smoke issuing from its chimney the engine hisses to a stop amid an aura of luxurious Victoriana. The last thing one expects to see emerging from such a train is a crowd of smartly besuited businessmen and office girls! This is Trindade, a haven of antiquity in a restless modern city: the trams rumble overhead, the tunnel entrance smokes and a delicate aroma of coffee from a nearby factory permeates the air. The Portuguese sunshine beats down and near the turntable an 0-4-4-0T Mallet quietly simmers between duties, its crew taking lunch in a nearby shady spot: peppers, Porto sardines and rolls or perhaps chicken and rice, with the inevitable flagons of wine which, incidentally, are usually carried in wicker baskets on the side of the locomotives. One would probably be invited to share the meal, such is the unparalleled friendliness of the Portuguese enginemen, and they never fail to be both amazed and proud that enthusiasts travel 1,500 miles to photograph their locomotives. Yes, Portugal may be a poor country, but its prevailing atmosphere of friendliness and simplicity is as enchanting as is its people's capacity to enjoy unsophisticated things. Such is Trindade, a place where engines gleam in the sunlight, faces smile and a pride of workmanship comes first.

When last at Trindade I took a train to Senhora and, owing to the heat, the coach windows were open. With a shriek from the Mallet's whistle we jerkedly started and as the rattling four-wheeled coaches entered the tunnel smoke 'puthered' in through a swirling blackness, window blinds flapped wildly and the silhouettes of other passengers could just be discerned through the dull orange glow of the carriage lamps. Far at the front the Mallet coughed its way through the tunnel with a whisping and spitting of steam that created polyphony with the exhaust beats. Victoriana lived again, sending one's imagination back in time to wander through the images of a past era until, upon bursting out into the sunshine, the rocking little coach with its hard wooden seats slowly cleared of smoke. A glance at the passengers showed them to be completely accustomed to all this and a glance through the window revealed new concrete flat blocks and one was forcibly reminded that this was the 20th century after all.

R.E.N.F.E. 242F Class 4–8–4   Pl. 23, 45

The final achievement in the R.E.N.F.E.'s range of standard giants came in the form of these superlative 4–8–4s known as Confederations. They are the only R.E.N.F.E. steam engines honoured with a green livery and invariably the class is beautifully maintained. All ten of them were built by Maquinista of Barcelona, the first in 1955 and the remaining nine in 1956. Breathtaking to see in action, they constitute the most impressive steam engines in Iberia and in terms of size and style they remind one of the ex-L.M.S.R. Princess Coronation class Pacifics – certainly the Princess Coronations were no more magnificent than these engines, although one does feel that a finishing touch would have been provided had they been given names.

These engines were built to cope with the increasingly heavy express trains between Avila and Alsasua (the section of line between Irun and Madrid which was not electrified), operation of the Iberia express being one of their principal duties. Their ability to haul heavy trains, often at high speeds, ensured a fine reputation amongst R.E.N.F.E. enginemen, who regarded them as Spain's foremost express steam engines. Other duties performed were the expresses between Miranda, Lerida and Mora, but despite their capabilities modernisation has caused them to be demoted and now the entire class is based at Miranda for working freight trains to Alsasua, Pamplona and Castejon.

The entire class was built to burn oil and among their other sophistications are double blast-pipes and chimneys, combined steam and vacuum brakes, turbo-generators for electric lighting and roller bearing axle boxes on all axles. Other features include O.C. Lentz Valves and boilers and fittings which are identical to those of the R.E.N.F.E.'s 1944 design 241Fs (see page 130). Leading dimensions are: 2 cylinders $25\frac{5}{16}''$ × $28''$, driving wheels 6' $2\frac{3}{4}''$ diameter, boiler pressure 227 lb per sq in, grate area 57 sq ft, axle loading $19\frac{1}{2}$ tons and the total weight in full working order is no less than 210 tons. Their oil and water-carrying capacities are 3,135 gallons and 6,170 gallons respectively.

Fortunately, the majority are still in service and in 1970 some received new driving wheels from which it may be assumed that the R.E.N.F.E. intend to keep the class in service for some time to come. Their attractive dark green livery is a distinction in itself, for these days very few main-line steam engines appear in anything other than black. Understandably they have become a principal attraction for railway enthusiasts and as the class is not especially overworked, a visit to Miranda depot will usually find a number of them, and what a contrast they make with the other R.E.N.F.E. types! When the last of these engines is withdrawn they will be remembered in the annals of locomotive history – for these 'Confederations' are one of the most interesting steam types left in the world today.

D.B. 044 Class 2-10-0 Pl. 24, 98

Although it was not until 1943 that the first British 2-10-0 design appeared, the type had been introduced in Germany as early as 1912. Ever since, 2-10-0s have played a very important role in German motive power and the study of their history makes a very fascinating subject. The first important ones were the 3-cylinder Prussian G12s which were built in large numbers from 1917, and by the time Germany's railways came under state control in 1920, some 1,350 were at work. These G12s became the D.R.B.'s 58 Class and owing to their success it was decided to feature 2-10-0s in the D.R.B.'s 'Locomotive Standardisation Plan'. Altogether some 284 different classes had been absorbed upon nationalisation and over the following years the D.R.B.

produced a scheme, with typical German efficiency, to reduce these to 29 standard classes.

Accordingly, in 1926, the D.R.B.'s first 2-10-0 heavy freight locomotives came into being: these were the 3-cylinder 44 Class which later became classified by the D.B. as 044. However, in 1927, a similar 2-cylinder design was produced, known as the 43 Class, with a view to comparing the two types, and initially only 10 engines of each design were built in order to determine the most economical methods of construction and operation. Both types received boilers similar to those of the 01 Pacifics, as Pacifics were also featured very extensively in this standardisation scheme. At higher outputs the 44 Class proved superior, but under prevailing circumstances, with a world trade recession causing only moderate loads, the 2-cylinder 43s were more favourable for the medium-power outputs required. This led to a further 25 43s being ordered, while the 44s remained at ten engines. However, upon the advent of more stimulated trading conditions, loads increased again, resulting in more 44s being built, while type 43 remained at 35 engines. From 1936 onwards 44s were built in vast numbers and their boiler pressure was increased from 206 lb per sq in to 235 lb per sq in. As Germany entered World War II the 44s became a reliable and valuable mainstay in moving the vast wartime loads. Accordingly, by 1945, little short of 2,000 had been constructed. Many were built in the works of occupied countries including Denmark, Austria and France; in this latter country they later became S.N.C.F. Class 150X, 90 of which were sold to the Turkish State Railways in 1958. As a result of wartime conditions some 44s were built in simplified 'U.K.' form (see page 128).

After the division of Germany's railways in 1945 distribution of the class occurred between the D.B. and the D.R. All the 43s, however, passed to the D.R., the last one being withdrawn in 1967, although one was earmarked for Dresden Transport Museum. The D.R. continued to build 44s up to 1949 and the total constructed over the years is in excess of 2,000.

The 44s' dazzling capabilities may be seen by their ability to haul 2,000-ton trains on level track at 35 m.p.h. and 1,000-ton trains up a 1 in 100 incline at 20 m.p.h. Another ability is their capacity to traverse curves of a 460' radius. Principal dimensions include 3 cylinders $21\frac{3}{8}'' \times 26''$, driving wheels 4' 7" diameter, grate area 49 sq ft, an axle loading of $19\frac{1}{2}$ tons and a tractive effort in excess of 60,000 lb. Coal and water capacities are $9\frac{3}{4}$ tons and 7,500 gallons respectively, the full weight of engine in working order is 112 tons and the total length 74'.

In 1955 the D.B. commenced tests with oil-firing and as a

result 32 Class 44s were so fitted. Under the recent D.B. renumbering scheme these became reclassified 043 and care must be taken not to confuse these with the old D.R.B. 43 Class of 1927.

Tests on the D.R. have led to some of their 44s being converted to oil-burning although many have been equipped with new welded boilers. On the D.B., in vivid contrast to the oil-burners, was the fitting of Mechanical Stokers to a few engines, but this innovation has never been favoured by the Germans and no examples remain today.

Along with their sisters, the 50s, the 44s have provided a magnificent mainstay in the German steam-fleet and further-more have become responsible for much of the best work obtained from steam power on today's D.B. They are by far the most powerful locomotives in Germany and amongst the most powerful in Europe. Despite heavy withdrawals they are well in evidence, several hundred still remaining in traffic, and it is hoped that many will survive for some years yet. Always exciting engines to watch, 44s are generally distri-buted throughout West Germany and trains in excess of 3,000 tons are frequently operated by double-heading, especially on the Mosel Valley route, where the gradients really put them through their paces. The sight and sound of two 44s tackling the climb out of Bullay is not easily for-gotten (see plate no. 98), and memories return of the halycon days of steam supremacy. The rough terrain of the Mosel Valley suits their character, their barking exhausts animating the wild setting. Some may also be found on the Münster–Emden route where, on occasions, they are paired with a 2–8–2 of Class 042, to work heavy hopper trains.

C.P. Metre Gauge Henschel 2–8–2T Nos 141–144   Pl. 25

Following the 1924 series of Henschel 2–8–2Ts for the Val do Vouga, page 169, the N.P. acquired four of these stately engines in 1931. They are decidedly larger than the V.V.'s engines and have two special distinctions: first, although over 40 years old, the class constitutes the last batch of steam engines built for the Portuguese metre gauge, and secondly they are the only metre-gauge type to possess smoke deflec-tors. Built for the lines radiating from Porto Trindade, these four engines still remain on their original territory and are usually found working the Póvoa route. They really enliven the metre-gauge system, their massive business-like appear-ance making a vivid contrast with some of the antiquities, and their bustling and powerful image is borne out by the class' rapid acceleration, and the high speeds reached between stations. The huge boilers lined with domes are unmis-takable and their superlative chime whistles add yet another
144   ring of character to the C.P. metre gauge. Quite apart from

the engines' up-to-date appearance the rakes of modern steel coaches used on the Póvoa service are radically different from the assorted conglomeration of four wheeled stock usually seen, and the sight of a 2–8–2T at speed with seven of these new coaches brings an air of modernity quite out of character with the remainder of the system. Usually the class works bunker first out of Porto, presumably because they are too large to turn at Póvoa.

The vibrant presence of these engines is accentuated when they emit voluminous rolls of rich brown smoke. Certainly all the metre-gauge engines have their moments in this respect, but all are beaten hands down by these 2–8–2Ts. To my delight I have seen Senhora da Hora quite blanketed out, while at the Trindade terminus the palls of smoke discharged skywards can be seen all over Porto.

All four engines are based at Boa Vista and their dimensions, which are as impressive as their appearance, may be summarised as follows: 2 cylinders $17\frac{3}{4}'' \times 23\frac{1}{2}''$, driving wheels 4' 5'' diameter, boiler pressure 171 lb per sq in, grate area 21 sq ft and a tractive effort at 75 per cent boiler pressure of no less than 21,936 lb – almost equivalent to the C.P. broad-gauge 4–6–0s! The class is superheated and is fitted with Kylala blast pipes; the effect of the engines' length is tempered by a lateral movement in the second and fourth coupled axles.

How long the 2–8–2Ts will survive is impossible to estimate, but in 1971 they were still being overhauled at Porto Campanhã works, as in fact were all metre-gauge classes and one ardently hopes that Portugal's metre-gauge steam will see some years of active service yet. Although no firm plans for metre-gauge modernisations have been announced, the number of engines, despite the variety, is not high and it is possible that a modernisation programme could be swiftly implemented and all steam swept away within a year or so; in this context the rapidity of the Spanish and British schemes must not be forgotten. However, owing to the diverse nature of the various metre-gauge routes and their traffic, perhaps combined with Portugal's status and temperament, rapid modernisation seems rather unlikely and possibly we might hope to see these 2–8–2Ts, along with the other engines of this remarkable system, for some years to come.

C.P. Metre Gauge Orenstein-Koppel 2–6–0T Nos E91–97
Pl. 28, 49, 63, 76, 86

This series of neat locomotives was built for the Val do Vouga Railway in 1910 and was numbered 1–7 by that company. Upon the V.V.'s absorption into the C.P. in 1947 the class became renumbered E91–97. The E prefix, which is an abbreviation of the Portuguese word 'Estreite', meaning narrow, has been added by the C.P. to all metre-gauge engines in order to distinguish them from the 5′ 6″ gauge locomotives. These engines have a short wheelbase and are eminently suitable for light passenger and freight work over twisting routes. All seven remain in traffic, six of which are on their system of origin being based at Sernada da Vouga and, as the colour plates indicate, they are heavily used on the Aviero line. One engine has, however, wandered to Boa Vista whilst another was for some time the only steam engine allocated to the 31-mile long Tâmega line. Most of the class, including those illustrated, were built by Orenstein and Koppel of Berlin, although three engines Nos 93/4/5 came from Decauville.

The Portuguese metre gauge may be divided into three sections: the lines radiating out of Porto Trindade station, the four feeder lines that intercept the Douro Valley route, and the system further south based on Sernada da Vouga. Sernada, the ex-V.V. Railway's headquarters, is little more than a sleepy village but is the focal point of a fascinating series of lines totalling some 140 miles. These lines are especially attractive and picturesque and their anatomy is shown by the map on page 160. At one time plans were afoot to connect the Sernada system with the Douro Valley by building a line from Viseu to Régua, thus providing metre-gauge operation between Chaves and Viseu, and onward via the 31-mile long Dão line to the famous wine area of Sta. Comba Dão whereupon the 5′ 6″ Beira Alta line to the Spanish frontier is joined. Such a scheme would also have given better access to Lisbon from the Douro Valley via Viseu, Sernada, Aveiro and thence down the electrified main line, thus avoiding the need to travel via Porto. Although some work was done on this project, including building a bridge over the River Douro at Régua, the idea has since been abandoned and there now seems scant likelihood of it ever materialising.

I have spent much time at Sernada as it is a place I find especially pleasant. Set in the remote Vouga Valley amid woodlands, the village resounds perpetually to locomotive whistles, for here are situated the old V.V. engine sheds and works, the former now having no less than five different kinds of tank engine allocated to them, including the four attractive Borsig 4–6–0Ts of 1908. At Sernada there are sufficient trains to keep interest at boiling point and when one begins to explore the delights of the various divergent lines the days quickly melt into weeks, since the Vouga Valley is one of those places bestowed with a glorious aspect of timelessness. Each line has its own individualities: the Viseu line with its dramatic scenery and viaducts, plate no. 87, the Espinho route spiralling away up the hillside through dense woodlands only to break out into soft undulating country-side as it heads towards the Atlantic coast, plate no. 30, and the meandering Aveiro line which upon leaving Sernada station crosses the beautiful stone viaduct over the Vouga Valley, plate no. 49.

On days when one is not exploring the lines, Sernada itself provides many gratifications: freshly caught and grilled fish are on sale in the little station buffet, presumably caught in the Vouga, and scrumptious locally grown oranges and pears are abundant. Sometimes I would sit alongside the Vouga Viaduct, plate no. 76, where I frequently met a little Portuguese boy with whom I exchanged words of our respective languages and although we could communicate little he was especially interested in the natural history book that I carried; he had a fine knowledge of his country's wildlife and enthusiastically pointed out a selection of mammals he had seen at Sernada.

Yes, despite what the protagonists say, steam railways do go with tranquillity, especially in this noisy relentless age, and where better to find them than Sernada: a restful village forgotten by everything except the steam age.

C.P. 4–6–2 Nos 551–560   Pl. 29

In 1924 Henschel delivered this class as a batch of ten pacifics to the S.S. division of Portugal's state railway and over many years they were the principal express engines south of the River Tagus. Modern in appearance and stately machines in every way, these 4-cylinder compounds are readily recognisable by their four domes. Another distinguishing feature is the situation of their outside cylinders which lie between the second bogie and the leading pair of driving wheels. Their large driving wheels and spokes are very slender and finely cast; these, when combined with the outside Walschaerts Valve Gear, give the engines a graceful appearance when running at speed, producing a fascinating tapestry of mechanism. The high-pressure cylinders are placed outside and the cut-offs to high and low-pressure cylinders are independent. The appearance of 'foreign' locomotives is often marred by too many domes, but these become infinitely less formidable when one can determine their use, and in the case of these Pacifics the first and third are sand boxes, the second the top feed cover, and the fourth contains the regulator.

Only one engine from this class now survives, No. 553, which is based at Contumil for working the Minho line between Porto Campanhã, Viana and Monção. Others were in service until recently and several lie derelict at Contumil depot. The ex-S.S. engines are one of Portugal's two Pacific classes, the other being a batch of eight engines built by

Henschel to the C.P.'s requirements in 1925 for working express trains on the main line between Porto and Lisbon. These engines were also 4-cylinder compounds and had the same cylinders and driving wheels; in fact the two types look almost identical. This class was numbered from 501 to 508 and after their complete withdrawal one engine, No. 501, was rather surprisingly reinstated to traffic in 1971, whereupon it commenced working between Porto and Régua. Its axle loading was too high to enable it to work east of that point. Imagine my incredulity when, during my visit to Régua in 1971, No. 501 suddenly turned up with a train from Porto; a living example from a class I had assumed to have been long withdrawn! Freshly overhauled, she looked resplendent in gleaming black livery, vivid red buffer beams, burnished buffers and sparkling brasswork. This locomotive's appearance in Régua extends even further the fine diversity of steam engines to be seen there. They range from metre-gauge 0–4–0Ts and 2–4–6–0T Mallets to broad-gauge 2–6–4Ts, 2–8–4Ts, 4–6–0s, 4–6–2s and 2–8–0s.

The use of 4-cylinder compound engines in Portugal has been widespread, especially with many older 4–6–0 types, as coal which had to be imported was both scarce and expensive. During the coal shortage in World War II many engines were reduced to burning wood, and a sequel to this has been the fitting for oil-burning of all Portuguese broad-gauge steam engines, with the exception of two diminutive 0–4–0T shed pilots. The leading dimensions of the ex-S.S. pacifics are: 4 cylinders, 2 H.P. $15'' \times 25\frac{1}{4}''$, 2 L.P. $22\frac{3}{4}'' \times 25\frac{1}{4}''$, driving wheel diameter 6' $2\frac{3}{4}''$, boiler pressure 228 lb per sq in, grate area $41\frac{1}{4}$ sq ft, tractive effort 22,435 lb and total weight in working order 145 tons.

How long these two surviving Pacifics will last is open to speculation as route limitations, owing to their axle weights, mean that they cannot fully participate in the lighter 4–6–0 diagrams. Their retention in service, however, adds a further attraction to Portugal's fascinating stud of broad-gauge locomotives.

R.S.H. 0–4–0ST

Pl. 32, 52

It seems strange that in the space of less than a decade, the status of the British steam locomotive should fall from such levels of working as the high-speed Anglo-Scottish runs to a few waggons around such installations as power stations, collieries and certain other industrial establishments. Nevertheless, it is in such environments that Britain's surviving steam locomotives are to be found.

The great majority of these 'industrial engines' had been built by private manufacturers and until recently a fascinating diversity of origins and designs could be found. Up until just a few years ago it was widely believed that industry would provide a spawning ground for steam power over many decades to come. Unfortunately, dieselisation, combined with the closure of many industrial railway systems, has decimated the ranks of the surviving engines and it now seems almost certain that extinction of the steam locomotive in Britain will occur sometime during the 1970s. In saying this I obviously exclude the special preservation establishments.

An effect of the continuing rundown of steam power has been to render the surviving engines increasingly obsolete: spare parts are no longer manufactured and therefore shopping facilities have become increasingly difficult and expensive. The setting up of smokeless zones has also influenced the decline in steam as indeed has the psychological factor that it is nowadays discredited by many authorities.

More tangible perhaps is the increasing use of 'Merry Go Round' trains whereby plants are served direct by British Rail and are thus able to dispense with the need for their own internal railway network. Many collieries and power stations are now adapted for this method of operating.

Such gloomy reflections, however, disperse rapidly when one thinks of the engines that can still be enjoyed, and although confined to small yards, they are none the less interesting than many of their main-line counterparts of years ago.

The locomotive illustrated in plate numbers 32 and 52 is a fine example of what might still be found in British industrial environments. Surprisingly, it was built as recently as 1950 by Robert Stephenson and Hawthorn of Newcastle-upon-Tyne, but the design dates back to the days of the Hawthorn Leslie Company, and it was one of their standard 12″ engines of which a considerable number have been built over the last 40 years or so.

This locomotive was purchased in order to cope with the increase in traffic at Leicester Power Station when, after nationalisation of the power industry in 1948, the Central Electricity Generating Board extended the operations there by installing two new turbo-generators. The duty of the engine is to take loaded coal waggons from the reception siding with B.R. and place them on the off-loading roads, whence they roll by gravity onto the tipplers adjacent to the main boiler plants. Each loaded train consists of eight 21-tonners. After the waggons are emptied, the locomotive returns them to the reception sidings.

The engine has two slide-valve cylinders of 12″ × 20″ operated by Stephenson's link motion, a boiler pressure of 160 lb per sq in, a heating surface of 402 sq ft and a fire grate

149

area of $6\frac{1}{2}$ sq ft. The saddle tank holds 500 gallons of water and the engine in full working order weighs 21 tons. Two live steam injectors are fitted for boiler feed requirements along with steam sanding gear and steam brakes.

Due to two of the power station's boilers now being fired by oil the reduced amount of coal traffic is currently handled by the station's two 0–4–0 fireless locomotives, but it is the C.E.G.B.'s intention to retain the engine in commercial use as a standby. The longevity of the R.S.H. 0–4–0ST has been aided by a complete re-tubing of the boiler in 1968 by the C.E.G.B. Central Workshops at Hams Hall, and continued protection is given by the use of distilled water, which is produced for the main boiler plants of the power station. In addition, the engine's boiler tubes have been fitted with ferrules at the fire-box tubeplate to prevent tube erosion by ash. Obviously the most expensive part of a locomotive is the boiler and nowadays a complete replacement would cost some thousands of pounds.

Despite the engine remaining in commercial use, the C.E.G.B. have already received some enquiries from potential purchasers for preservation, and with a scrap price of little over £200 it seems almost certain that when her working days finally end, someone will add her to the ever-growing ranks of preserved British industrial engines. I, for one, certainly hope so.

Other locomotives of the same design may still be found in service with the Northern Gas Board at Redheugh Works, Gateshead.

Kitson 0–6–0ST   Pl. 35

Over recent years one of the most delightful attractions for steam enthusiasts in Britain was the various ironstone railways of Northamptonshire. In the picturesque countryside, for which Northamptonshire is noted, many fascinating engines could be found at work. These ironstone systems possessed an atmosphere and character almost impossible to describe: they were rustic, friendly, quaint and yet dramatic, and gave railway enthusiasts, if not the local population in general, a tangible compensation for the many acres of land put asunder by the mineral workings. Looking back on these systems, I feel a deep sense of loss, for their priceless character is totally irreplaceable. The industrial lines which survive today are, in the main, too heavily industrialised, with much of the running being confined to sidings, whilst our nearest alternative, the preserved lines, wonderful though they are, inevitably cannot provide that stimulation created by what one might call 'the elusive air of the authentic', which is so vital to enthusiasts the world over. I speak retrospectively of these lines, because rationalisations within the steel industry, combined with a decline in demand for home-produced iron-ore in favour of imported iron-ore, has resulted in many of them being closed, while those that remain are now fully dieselised.

Storefield, perhaps the most charming of these rural systems, is the subject of plate no. 35. Set over a mile from the nearest habitation, it lies amid woodlands and glades teeming with nature. Quarrying began early this century but the workings lapsed during the depression and were closed in 1929. However, during World War II, when the production of large quantities of home-produced iron-ore became essential, the South Durham Steel and Iron Co., who had since acquired the quarrying rights, recommenced operations. Almost a mile long, the line connects the quarries with B.R.'s main Kettering to Manton route.

For many years, four steam locomotives were required for working the traffic, but in the late 1960s, when one of the two pits closed, only two engines were necessary for operating a weekly yield of some 3,000 tons. This continued until 1969 when a Rolls-Royce Sentinel diesel arrived and spelled the end of steam working.

Storefield had for long been noted for its vintage Barclay/Bagnall 0–4–0STs and after these were withdrawn the Kitson 0–6–0ST illustrated arrived from Stewart and Lloyds, having been made redundant by dieselisation. Named *Caerphilly,* she was Kitson No. 5477, built at their Leeds works in 1936. This engine arrived in August, 1968 to end its days at Storefield, until it was finally broken up by Cohens of Kettering in the Fall of 1969.

Caerphilly belonged to an interesting family of engines since originally the design was by Manning Wardle and Company of Leeds, who produced the first one in 1912. After perpetuating the design as a standard until 1926, Mannings closed down, and Kitson and Company, another Leeds locomotive builder, took over their goodwill and continued the design to order. Upon Kitson's demise in 1938, their drawings were acquired by Robert Stephenson and Hawthorn, who again built to the original pattern as required. Stewart and Lloyds, upon whose ironstone systems the type was immensely popular, ordered examples from all three builders with very little departure from the original design. The dimensions were 2 inside cylinders 16″ × 22″, driving wheel diameter 3′ 6″, boiler pressure 160 lb per sq in and a grate area of 14 sq ft. Coal and water capacities were $1\frac{1}{4}$ tons and 800 gallons respectively and the total weight in full working order was 38 tons.

Apart from the class's popularity with ironstone crews, steam preservationists have found them no less attractive and about six have been preserved. Their relatively small size renders them an ideal subject for preservationists with limited funds, and amongst those preserved is the last Manning Wardle engine No. 2047 of 1926, which the Severn Valley Railway acquired from the Rugby Portland Cement Co. Other examples may be found on the Railway Preservation Society's premises at Chasewater.

Some compensation for Storefield's passing may be found on a 12″ long-playing record released by President Records entitled 'The Storefield Story'. This is a plaintive account which evocatively recalls the line's day to day happenings. Featured on it are most of the older 0–4–0STs used on the line, along with *Caerphilly* and other associated ironstone sounds, although Storefield's noted 'steam digger' had, unfortunately, been rendered defunct prior to the recording being made. To the privileged few who knew the line this record is indispensable, and yet it conjures up so deep a sadness, if not a longing, for that which is no more, as to inevitably militate against one's pleasure.

Bagnall 0–6–0ST   Pl. 97

Another delightful line, similar in many respects to Storefield, was the Cranford ironstone system which lay only a few miles across country in a south-easterly direction. This system, owned by Staveley Minerals Ltd, was in operation until August, 1969 and became noted for its 1924 Avonside 0–6–0ST and 1941 Bagnall 0–6–0STs. Quarrying commenced at Cranford in the 1880s; originally the railway system was laid to metre gauge, but upon its conversion to standard gauge during the 1920s, an Avonside 0–6–0ST, named *Cranford,* was put to work. This type, which had squarish tanks, along with copper-capped chimney, was like several used by Staveley Minerals for ironstone work.

During World War II the Ministry of Supply commissioned six 15″ outside-cylinder 0–6–0STs from William Bagnall of Stafford, three of them for work in the Staveley Company's ironstone pits. The engine illustrated is *Cranford No. 2,* W. B. No. 2668, built in 1942. It has 2 inside cylinders 15″ × 22″, a driving wheel diameter of 3′ 4½″, a boiler pressure of 180 lb per sq in, a grate area of 13¾ sq ft and a 10′ wheelbase. The tanks hold 800 gallons of water, the axle loading is 13 tons whilst the total weight in working order is 39 tons.

Only seven engines of this type were constructed, the first in 1934, and no less than four of them have been preserved. *Cranford No. 2* is now at the Somerset and Dorset Railway Circle, Radstock, whilst another of the class adorns Daventry town centre.

Cranford, in common with Storefield, was one of the last ironstone lines in the country to hold steam power, which it did long after many of the famous ones had either been closed or dieselised. Its mile-long route connected up with B.R.'s Kettering to Cambridge line, which, after closure, was maintained from Kettering to Islip to facilitate conveyance of the ironstone. Always 100 per cent steam-operated, Cranford was set in deep countryside, and apart from the attraction of the various 0-6-0STs, there were the wild strawberries, which in summer grew in profusion along the tracksides. Little now remains of Cranford's defunct workings, and as nature takes its toll, it will become eventually just another vague earthwork. Fortunately, brilliant testimonials of Cranford still exist in its preserved engines, one of which is the celebrated 1891 Manning Wardle 0-6-0ST *Sir Berkeley,* currently gracing the Keighley and Worth Valley Railway at Haworth.

C.P. 2–6–4T 070–097/C.P. 2–8–4T 0181–0190   Pl. 42, 77

These handsome and solidly built 2–6–4 tank engines are by far the most numerous steam type in Portugal and may be seen principally on passenger services northwards from Porto's Campanhã station. Additionally, they have almost full operation of both the heavily-trafficked Nine to Braga branch and the Lexioés line, and they are also used along the Douro Valley route as depicted in plate no. 42. A further duty entrusted to them is the working of certain passenger trains from Porto Campanhã southwards along the electrified Lisbon main line as far as Espinho. This journey involves their crossing one of Porto's landmarks: M. Eiffel's lovely Maria Pia bridge of 1877, which carries the main line over the Douro to the south of Campanhã station. This bridge, which is 300 ft high, is so magnificent that it is featured on many of Porto's picture postcards – often with a 2–6–4T going over it!

These engines, introduced onto the C.P. in 1916, were Swiss-designed and built, fifteen being delivered from S.L.M. between 1916 and 1920. This batch, which bears today's number series 071–085, is especially distinctive in being one of the very few locomotive types ever exported from Switzerland. In 1929 a further twelve engines came from the German firm of Henschel. These were amongst a batch of locomotives supplied as war reparation in recognition of the Portuguese division that fought in France during World War I. The final engine to this design was built as late as 1944 and is equally interesting as it is the C.P.'s only Portuguese-built engine. Numbered 070, it was built to the same specifications as the others by Gerais of Lisbon. Portugal has never had any locomotive manufacturers of its own, so number 070 makes a sharp contrast to the multitude of French, German and British engines for which the country has become so noted.

Although maids of all work, these 2–6–4Ts were originally

built for the C.P.'s intensive suburban services out of Lisbon and Porto, along with a number of semi-fast trains between the two cities. Accordingly, their side tanks were supplemented by well tanks situated beneath the main frames, and this arrangement enabled them to carry over 2,000 gallons of water. However, electrification has largely ousted them from these duties and all survivors are now based at Porto Contumil depot.

They are remarkably lively and, despite their size, almost fussy engines, but once given the road they have no difficulty in building up brisk speeds between stops. Immensely popular with the engine crews, the class is exquisitely maintained, special attention being paid to their brass boiler bands and number plates. Very few examples have been withdrawn from service despite modernisations creating a shortage of work befitting their abilities. They have 2 outside cylinders $20\frac{1}{2}'' \times 25\frac{3}{16}''$, driving wheels of 5' 0" diameter, a boiler pressure of 171 lb per sq in, a grate area of $27\frac{1}{2}$ sq ft and a tractive effort of 22,540 lb. Their axle loading is 16 tons and the total weight in working order 80 tons.

The larger companions of the 2–6–4Ts are a batch of impressive 2–8–4Ts, ten of which were built by Henschel for the old S.S. division of the State Railways in 1925. Originally used in the south of Portugal, modernisations have since moved them northwards and now, in common with the 2–6–4Ts, all are based at Porto Contumil depot, with the exception of one engine which is allocated to Régua. In 1923 Henschel provided the C.P. with 24 similar but larger 2–8–4Ts, principally for freight workings on the Lisbon to Porto main line. These engines have since disappeared, presumably owing to their axle loadings being too high for use on other lines, and all the C.P.'s 2–8–4Ts today are from this ex-S.S. series, nine of which remain in traffic.

These 2–8–4Ts may be seen working northwards out of Campanhã, also between Nine and Braga and along the Minho line as far as Viana. Until recently a number were based at Régua for working the Douro Valley line but these have now been replaced by the 4–6–0s, except the one engine mentioned which Régua appears to use as a standby. The presence of this engine at Régua adds to the range of types seen there and provides a welcome locomotive variety to compensate for the rather sparse service between Régua and the Spanish border at Barca d'Alva. During my stay in the valley in 1971, this engine was working along with the 4–6–0s and took some turns on the famous 6.50 morning 'mixed' between Régua and Pocinho. The 2–8–4Ts leading dimensions are: 2 outside cylinders $20\frac{1}{2}'' \times 25\frac{3}{4}''$, driving wheel diameter 4' $5\frac{1}{4}''$, grate area $32\frac{1}{2}$ sq ft, tractive effort 27,190 lb and total weight in working order 109 tons.

It is difficult to estimate how long these two types will remain at work because a few years ago the C.P. announced its intention to dispense with all broad-gauge steam in 1970. Mercifully this did not take place and in fact over the last few years very little change in the status of steam has occurred – a fact which renders Portugal markedly different from every other European country! At present the C.P. have 60 broad-gauge (5′ 6″) steam engines in active service; not a large figure and one that could, in theory, be fairly quickly dispensed with. Although only a few engines remain, they are made up of no less than ten completely different types, all of which are maintained in impeccable condition. The diversity ranges from such delights as Beyer Peacock 2–6–2Ts of 1890 to German built 4-cylinder compound Pacifics of 1924.

One of the fundamental reasons for steam's retention in Portugal is the axle load restrictions north of Viana on the Minho line and east of Régua on the Douro Valley line. These restrictions prohibit use of the C.P.'s diesels and oblige them to use their more lightly-loaded steam engines, and until all the bridges, which are the cause of these restrictions, can be upgraded, it seems reasonable to hope that steam power will be retained. Work has commenced on this upgrading but there remains much to do yet; notwithstanding this, the C.P. expect to have eliminated broad-gauge steam traction by 1973.

One hopes fervently that it might continue for longer, for although much of Portugal's exotica has recently disappeared, it still remains, for the steam enthusiast, one of Europe's most worthwhile countries; when its metre-gauge lines are considered as well it becomes in the eyes of many second to none. Whatever the future of broad-gauge steam in Portugal, one may expect to see some of these 2–6–4Ts/2–8–4Ts at the fore until the very end.

Ex-R.E.N.F.E. 0–6–0 'Eslava'/Turon 2–4–0T 'Bilbao'
Pl. 43, 53, 64

By general standards in Western Europe Spain is a poor country; its economy largely relies upon fruit, wines, various mineral resources and, in more recent years, tourism. If adverse weather conditions affect the crops, the economy is disrupted; accordingly, the money available for such public expenditures as railway modernisations becomes limited. Furthermore, many rail services operating in Spain are very uneconomical but their retention as a social service is considered vital.

Modernisations could not progress very swiftly under such conditions, but when the Spanish Civil War broke out in 1936 it both thwarted and retarded any modernisation plan that might have been envisaged, rendered immense destruc- 155 tion to the railways and left Spain an almost impoverished country. In fact the effect of this war was such that of 3,146 serviceable locomotives available in 1936 only 1,837 were usable in 1939 when the war ended. Rehabilitation from such a state of affairs was hampered by World War II, and for some years Spain placed an emphasis on keeping its railways going rather than modernising. Modernisation, however, had been proceeding for many years, for the first electrification was completed in 1911. Thus, by the mid '60s, Spain was becoming widely noted for its ancient engines, which, in their vast numbers, were inextricably mixed with the incoming diesels and electrics. However, with American aid plus a considerably improved national economy, the R.E.N.F.E. has recently made immense strides both in motive power modernisation and in the building of new direct routes – the latter a particularly refreshing fact in these days of 'road mania'. By 1971, to all intents and purposes, the antiquities had disappeared.

Certainly this is the impression, but it is with relief that I record the existence of a fascinating complexity of loco-motive types and origins among Spain's secondary railways. These railways range from private narrow-gauge lines like the 'La Robla' to purely industrial systems such as the Rio Tinto complex or the Ponferrada–Villablino line (see page 133). Accumulatively such systems, and indeed many smaller ones, provide a wide number of locomotives of different gauges, despite modernisations and closures having taken their toll. Perhaps one of Spain's finest districts for steam-operated industrial lines is in Asturias (an area of the north-west part of the country). During my visit there in 1971, I found five different steam-worked gauges in use along with as fine a variety of engines as one could wish for, the best being an ex-N.O.R.T.E. 0–8–0 of 1879.

I made a base at Mieres, some 11 miles south of Oviedo, having made the journey to this isolated area over the 4,481' high Pajares pass through Sierra de Casomera, the tops of which were covered in snow. The area around Mieres puts one in mind of what Britain might have been like at the beginning of the industrial revolution, for the adjacent valleys are full of bitter-sweet intrigue. Coal mines and scattered hamlets vie with the natural beauty, in one glance enhancing it with a blended contrast, but in another desecrating it with the depression of industrial sprawl. Here in the valleys exists a profusion of industrial lines connecting collieries and washeries; here the mountain streams run black with coal dust; and here the steam age lives on.

Plate no. 43 depicts an ex-R.E.N.F.E. type in the form of an 0–6–0 tender engine. This priceless piece of locomotive history is currently used by Sociedad Hullera Espanola S.A., a company formed in 1892 to take over coal mining in the Aller Valley between Ujo and Moreda. The system's focal point is centered upon the screens at Ujo, and apart from its standard 5' 6" gauge, a 600-mm gauge line runs up the valley serving several mines en route. Despatch of coals is facilitated by the network's broad gauge connecting up with the R.E.N.F.E. electrified Leon to Oviedo main line. The engine's history is worthy of some comment, as originally she was built for passenger work on the Asturias–Galicia–Leon Railway (A.G.L.) by Richard Hartman & Co. of Chemnitz, Germany, in 1881, and acquired the name *Eslava*. In 1890, the A.G.L. was absorbed into the N.O.R.T.E., upon which *Eslava* worked for over fifty years before passing into R.E.N.F.E. stock in 1941, classified 030 2441. Her wanderings far from completed, she graduated onto Hullera de Turon's colliery system at Turon, and then a further move found her hard at work at Ujo in 1971. *Eslava* was one of thirty-seven similar engines built in Germany between 1881 and 1883, several of which still survive in various facets of Spanish industry including some at Fabrica de Mieres steelworks, Mieres. *Eslava* has 2 outside cylinders 18" × 24½", driving wheels 4' 7½" diameter and in full working order she weighs 63 tons. The engine, in common with other Spanish 0–6–0s has Allan Straight Link Motion.

Plate no. 53 shows a scene on one of the busiest centres in the area, Hulleras de Turon's colliery complex at Turon, which is a converging point for a number of mines situated in the Rio Turon Valley. Established in 1890, this system also connects with the R.E.N.F.E.'s Leon to Oviedo route by a 1½-mile broad-gauge line. Until recently this company operated three gauges: 600 mm, metre and broad 5' 6", but when I made my visit, the metre gauge appeared to be defunct. The 600-mm gauge line continues eastwards from Turon for some miles serving several drift mines en route and it is fascinating to watch these engines bringing loaded trains into Turon yards where, after emptying into the screens, the coal is transferred to broad-gauge waggons for the main shunting and exchange traffic. Having deposited their loads, the 600-mm engines storm their way back to the mines with empties. Depicted on the plate is *Bilbao,* a 5' 6" 2–4–0T, shunting the yard along with a derelict 600-mm 0–4–0T built by H. K. Porter Loco. Works Pittsburg, U.S.A. in 1913. This was one of a batch of earlier 600-mm engines delivered to Turon, most of today's traffic being hauled by 0–6–0Ts constructed by A.H.V., a Bilbao steel company in the 1940s.

Little is known about *Bilbao* – also featured on plate no. 64. She is numbered 103 and was supposedly built at Turon in 1921, but almost certainly parts of older locomotives were used in her construction and her ancient lineage would strongly suggest this. *Bilbao's* mysterious background probably renders her unique but despite her somewhat bastard origin she performs the duties with considerable relish and efficiency. It is unusual to find tank engines of the 2–4–0 type today and especially to find one in such an attractive green and red livery; certainly *Bilbao* is one of the most interesting engines extant in Spanish industry.

I found several other enthralling engines at Turon including a Sharp Stewart 2–4–0T of 1888 which, amazing as it may sound, was undergoing a complete overhaul in the Turon company's well-equipped workshops. In a later volume of this series I hope to include some further examples of Spain's vast abundance of industrial steam before this, like so many other good things, disappears under the umbrella of industrial rationalisation.

C.P. 2 cylinder 2–8–0 Nos 701–719   Pl. 44, 57, 84

The bulk of steam-hauled freight traffic in Portugal is handled by this class of 2-cylinder simple 2–8–0s with plate frames. The first eleven were supplied to the S.S. Railway from Schwartzkopf of Berlin, of which Nos 701–706 were delivered in 1912, followed by Nos 707–711 in 1913. A further eight engines of the same design were added in 1921 by the North British Locomotive Co., Glasgow. This class must not be confused with Portugal's other 2–8–0 type, the 4-cylinder ex-M.D. engines which are discussed on page 163.

Of the nineteen built, thirteen remained in traffic during 1971. All based at Porto Contumil depot, and with a light-axle loading of only $13\frac{3}{4}$ tons, they are to be found working freight on all the C.P.'s steam-worked lines, including some trips on the electrified Lisbon main line as far as Aviero. Also, in common with Contumil's other engines, they work under the wires on the Minho line which is electrified to San Romão – see map on page 160. One of the class's principal duties is working freight along the sinuous 12-mile branch from the large artificial port of Lexioés. This line heads westwards off the Minho route a little to the south of Contumil depot.

Unlike the C.P.'s other 2–8–0s, the class is superheated and has 2 outside cylinders $22'' \times 24\frac{3}{4}''$, driving wheels of $4' 4\frac{3}{8}''$ diameter, a boiler pressure of 171 lb per sq in, a grate area of $30\frac{1}{2}$ sq ft and a tractive effort at 75 per cent boiler pressure of 29,412 lb. Its total weight in full working order is 115 tons.

I have already referred to these engines as being ex-S.S. while the 4-cylinder 2–8–0s are ex-M.D. and this may be an opportune moment to discuss briefly the background of Portugal's broad-gauge railways in order that these locomotives, along with other Portuguese engines mentioned, may be seen in clearer perspective. Half of Portugal's broad-gauge (5′ 6″) mileage was owned and operated by the Portuguese Railway Company (C.P.), a company largely financed in France. This company built the Lisbon to Porto main line. Most of the country's other lines were state-owned; the largest of these were the Sul e Sueste (S.S.), which operated south of the river Tagus, and the Minho e Douro (M.D.), which covered the north and east of Porto. Another important provate line was the Beira Alta, but no loco-motives originating from this railway are illustrated in this volume and none are extant today although the company's old main line is connected at Sta Comba Dão with the Sernada metre-gauge system – see map on page 160.

In 1927 the C.P. obtained a lease to operate all state-owned railways; twenty years later it additionally incorpor-ated the Beira Alta; and today it is responsible for the operation of all Portuguese railways, excluding the short, electrified Estoril. This latter incorporation also unified the metre-gauge lines (see page 174) and was the culmination of a policy to merge the railways under one management to increase overall efficiency.

Ex-M.Z.A., R.E.N.F.E. 240F Class 4–8–0
Pl. 46, 62, 68, 88, 100

The ending of the Spanish Civil War in 1939 left Spain's railways in a devastated and run-down condition and the almost concurrent outbreak of World War II meant that little help could be expected from other countries. It became obvious that government action was essential if the railways were to survive and accordingly 1 February, 1941 saw the Spanish broad-gauge (5′ 6″) railways nationalised. Thus the R.E.N.F.E. was created. Altogether the state system incorpor-ated some twenty-two companies, the four major ones being N.O.R.T.E. – Northern Railway of Spain, M.Z.A. – Madrid, Zaragoza and Alicante Railway, ANDALUCES – Andalusian Railways, and the O.E.S.T.E. – National Western Railway. The M.Z.A. covered important cities in southern, central and north-eastern parts of Spain and was the first railway to start a long tradition of 4–8–0 engines in the country with their famous 1912 design from Henschel of Germany, to which 127 engines were built up to 1921. The establishment of 4–8–0s in Spain fulfilled some very basic needs, because the difficult terrain had always imposed a restriction on permitted axle loadings and the 4–8–0 arrangement provided excellent adhesion yet enabled axle loads to be light in relation to the power output. Having produced a powerful engine within the specified axle loading, a general policy of few but heavy trains could be adopted, and within a few years 4–8–0s became a prolific type of the principal companies for the more import-ant passenger and freight duties.

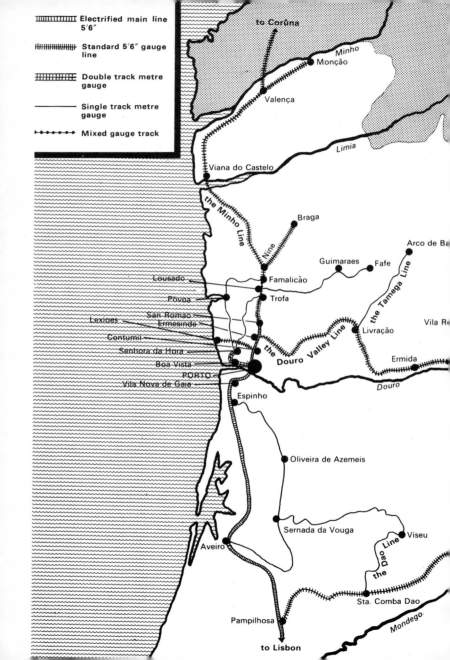

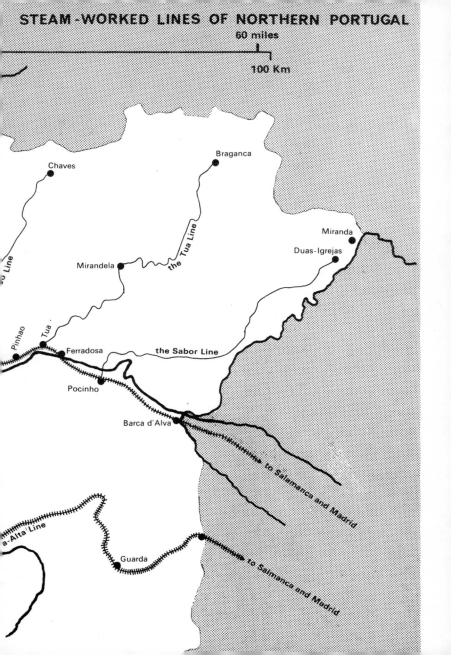

STEAM-WORKED LINES OF NORTHERN PORTUGAL

60 miles

100 Km

Chaves

Braganca

Miranda

Duas-Igrejas

Mirandela

the Tua Line

Pinhao

Tua

Line

Ferradosa

the Sabor Line

Pocinho

Barca d'Alva

to Salamanca and Madrid

a-Alta Line

Guarda

to Salamanca and Madrid

Success with their 4–8–0s induced the M.Z.A. to order a further batch of 165 engines which were built between 1920 and 1931 and, although having some resemblance to the 1912 design, the new engines were bigger and more powerful. They were known as the M.Z.A. 1400 Class, and this is the type illustrated. So successful were they, that similar engines were built for the ANDALUCES from 1926 and the O.E.S.T.E. from 1932. This resulted in some 300 almost identical engines appearing, and it is fascinating to record that six more were built as late as 1947 for use in Portugal where they worked on the C.P.'s Zone 3, becoming their 831 Class. These six engines are believed to be Spain's only steam locomotive exports.

Another absorbing fact about the 1400s is that they were one of the forerunners of an emerging school of Spanish design. Until the 1920s, Spain's locomotives were supplied principally by Germany, France, Great Britain and Belgium, but the 1400s were Spanish-designed and built by the now famous firm, Maquinista of Barcelona. The entire M.Z.A. batch came from their works. In fact this order constituted the largest ever placed with one builder by any Spanish railway company and it makes an interesting contrast with the 38 O.E.S.T.E. engines which were built between 1932/40 when four builders were used; Maquinista, Euskalduna of Bilbao, Babcock & Wilcox of Bilbao, and Macosa of Valencia, whilst the ANDALUCES engines, built between 1926/42, came from Maquinista and Devis of Valencia. As may be realised, it was typically Spanish practice to allocate the building of any given class to several different firms, often in different countries.

Over the years certain variations occurred within the 1400s; noteworthy amongst these were the twenty engines built for the M.Z.A. between 1936 and 1940 with Lentz valve gear, smoke deflectors and enlarged tenders, and although these differed in appearance they were ostensibly identical to the remainder of the class. In 1925 the M.Z.A. produced an exciting enlargement of a 1400 in the form of a 4–8–2. Apart from their size these engines looked much the same and had many dimensions in common. Designed for express passenger work they were, along with a N.O.R.T.E. Class of the same year, Spain's first 4–8–2s and as such heralded a widespread use of that type throughout Spain (see page 130).

In 1935 the ANDALUCES railway perpetuated the 4–8–0 tradition by introducing a further design which was taken up by the O.E.S.T.E. and M.Z.A. after the Civil War, although these engines were absorbed immediately by the R.E.N.F.E. who continued to order them from Spanish builders until 1953 when, upon the R.E.N.F.E. commissioning their 141Fs, further construction ceased (see page 117). The only surviving

4-8-0s on today's R.E.N.F.E. are some 1400s and a few M.Z.A./R.E.N.F.E. survivors of the 1935 ANDALUCES design, and visitors to Spain may readily distinguish the latter type by their massive windshields and, in many instances, double chimneys. These two locomotive types bear a scattered testimonial to Spain's wide usage of 4-8-0s, and it is expected that at least a handful will survive for a year or two yet. The 1400s' leading dimensions may be summarised as: 2 cylinders $24\frac{3}{8}'' \times 26''$, driving wheels 5' 3" diameter, boiler pressure 199 lb per sq in, grate area 49 sq ft, and axle loading $15\frac{1}{2}$ tons. The total weight of the locomotive in full working order is 140 tons.

Having worked all over the R.E.N.F.E. system apart from the former N.O.R.T.E. and 'Central Aragon' lines, the 1400s have become a popular and ubiquitous class. Their presence is one of the principal pleasures on today's R.E.N.F.E., for although the last ten years have seen an immense run down of Spanish steam, examples of these big engines are still active along with some even bigger 4-8-2s and 4-8-4s (see pages 130 and 141). All these designs have a distinct and palatable Spanish aura and they offer tangible compensation for the recent passing of the many antiquities which attracted so many locomotive enthusiasts to Spain. A good area to catch the 1400s in action is on the lines radiating out of Salamanca, and although this town lies some way west of Spain's principal steam belt around Miranda, the journey is well worthwhile, for few enthusiasts could fail to experience a thrill upon seeing a fifty-year-old 4-8-0 in full action, especially when it is a survivor from so great a tradition. At the time of writing no plans have been made for the preservation of a 1400, but an example of the similar ex-M.Z.A. 4-8-0s of 1912 is set by for incorporation in Spain's Railway Museum.

C.P. Metre Gauge Kessler 0-6-0T Nos E51-56   Pl. 47

In 1889 Emil Kessler of Germany supplied six of these 0-6-0 tank engines to the C.N. for use on their 33 mile long Dão line upon which they were numbered 1-6. The Dão line is an important link between the V.V. system at Viseu and the 5' 6" gauge Beira Alta main line at Sta. Comba Dão. Unlike many Portuguese metre-gauge engines, this type has become rather scattered from its original haunts, four of the class now being based at Tua for shunting and operations on the Tua line. One of these engines, No. E52, is named *Viseu* in deference to its origins and as such it is the only named Portuguese locomotive; this engine is well worth seeing as its highly-coloured nameplate and polished brasswork render it especially attractive. Apart from the four Tua engines another is dumped at Boa Vista whilst E54 lies out of use at   163

Régua where, until 1971, it was actively engaged upon station pilot duties. Its place has now been taken by E1, a diminutive Henschel 0–4–0T of 1922.

However, the four Tua engines are highly active and along with the remarkable Kessler 2–6–0Ts of 1886 (page 122), with which they share the workings, they add a unique touch of character to the Tua line. Their gaunt angular chimneys, massive domes and distinctively-shaped buffer beams are typical of Portugal's Kessler-built engines, but in addition these 0–6–0Ts have backless cabs, which give them a strange, cut-away appearance. The use of these two types on the Tua line makes that route the most interesting of the four Douro Valley feeder systems, because upon the Corgo and Sabor lines the more recent 2–4–6–0T Mallets have a virtual monopoly of traffic, whilst the Tâmega line sees but little steam working, what there is being handled by one of the original 0–4–4–0T Mallets which were originally delivered in 1905 for the N.P.

Tua is situated $87\frac{1}{2}$ miles from Porto at the confluence of the Tua and Douro (see plate no. 59). The place itself is little more than a sleepy hamlet whose sole significance lies in its situation at the meeting point of the main Douro line and the 83-mile long Tua line to Mirandela and the historic town of Bragança in the most north-easterly corner of Portugal. It does however possess one other point of interest, which is recognised primarily by railway enthusiasts, in that it provides a meeting place for these ancient Kessler metre-gauge tank engines and 60-year-old broad-gauge 4–6–0s.

Upon leaving Tua the metre-gauge line enters the precipitous Tua Valley over a viaduct built into the hillside followed immediately afterwards by a tunnel; thence it runs through the wildness of the Tua gorge for some 25 miles. This route necessitated the construction of numerous bridges, tunnels and viaducts and was opened to Mirandela in 1887, finally reaching Bragança in 1906. Several times daily these delightful little tank engines traverse the line hauling their mixed trains of passengers, mail, wine, fruit and general produce.

When visiting Tua I am reluctant to wander far along the main Douro Valley line for fear of missing activity on the metre gauge and often I choose a spot just inside the Tua Valley which affords a view of both lines; at this point the metre-gauge line curves out of the gorge to run to the station, and the last $\frac{1}{4}$ mile runs alongside the main line which approaches from the west over the Tua Viaduct (see plate no. 21). Tua, in accord with other junctions in the Valley, has periodical bursts of activity as most trains are timed to connect. Additionally it serves as a crossing point on the single tracked Douro Valley line and it is possible, at certain times, to see the two Kessler-design tank engines along with

both types of broad-gauge 4–6–0 in the station simultane-
ously. In contrast, gaps of several hours occur between trains
and during this time one may relax in the warm sunshine or
enjoy a quiet drink in the tiny store attached to the station.
Oftentimes I would amuse myself with a pet monkey who
lived in a tree at the eastern end of the station. He was a
sprightly little fellow, well known to all the locomotive crews
who would throw titbits to him as the trains passed. Unfortunately upon my last visit he was nowhere to be seen and
the waiting time at Tua now seems that little bit lonelier
without his presence.

C.P. 4-cylinder Compound 2–8–0 Nos 751–766 Pl. 50, 65, 79

Four-cylinder compound 2–8–0s have never been a commonplace type but in Portugal they are just another fascinating variety amid the C.P.'s steam fleet. This remarkable series
of engines originated in 1912 on the State Railway's Minho
and Douro division, the first four being built in that year by
the North British Locomotive Co. of Glasgow. Later a
further twelve to the same specifications were supplied
between 1913 and 1924 by Schwarzkopf of Berlin. The class
has bar frames and coned boilers but more noticeable is the
remarkably high pitch of the boilers and this leaves a wide
space between boiler and frame, which is of course ideal for
accessibility when servicing the inside motion. Plate no. 79
shows this very clearly and in this aspect these engines were
well ahead of their years; certainly in Britain it was not until
the mid-1940s that such features were introduced. It is this
high footplating which gives them a strong American
flavour, for it was in that country that the provision of
accessibility was carried to its utmost from an early date.
The massive outside cylinders are another noteworthy
feature and as one may imagine these are the low-pressure
ones (see plate no. 65). One important 'sophistication' not
included, however, is super-heating, rather surprisingly as
the 2-cylinder 2–8–0s of the same period incorporate this
innovation.

Only one engine now survives from the original fifteen;
this is No. 754 based at Contumil for freight duties, and
although it works turn about with the other 2–8–0s it may
frequently be seen on the heavy overnight mixed train from
Porto to Régua. Quite a number of withdrawn examples may
be found dumped at Contumil and Vila Nova de Gaia. This
engine, along with two surviving pacifics, brings to an end
Portugal's long tradition of 4-cylinder compound broad-
gauge engines. Although by no means large, No. 754 has
some very adequate proportions: the cylinders are 2 H.P.
$14\frac{1}{4}'' \times 25\frac{1}{2}''$, 2 L.P. $23\frac{1}{4}'' \times 25\frac{1}{2}''$, driving wheel diameter 4′
$3\frac{1}{4}''$, boiler pressure 228 lb per sq in, grate area 38 sq ft,

tractive effort 31,330 lb and the total weight in full working order is 125 tons.

Whether it is the inevitable thrill attached to sole survivors or just that 4-cylinder compound 2–8–0s are so unusual is difficult to say, but the movements of No. 754 are well plotted by visiting enthusiasts and she is one of the C.P.'s most frequently pursued locomotives. My first acquaintance with her was one lunchtime at Régua while waiting for the overnight mixed to arrive from Porto. As the train came into sight a call went up, 'it's the compound', and sure enough into view came this strange, chubby 2–8–0. It headed gently over the embankment with its heavy train until a sudden burst of acceleration necessitated a dash of oil onto the fire and out came a pall of inky black smoke; plate no. 79 shows this scene. Since that time No. 754 has become a firm favourite of mine and I have been fortunate enough to see her many times during the course of my visits to Portugal.

R.S.H. 0–4–0CT   Pl. 54, 74, 75

The *Sunderland Echo* of Friday, 18 December, 1970 carried a heading 'The old Pallion yard workhorses to retire' and thus heralded the end of an important tradition in British locomotive history. The heading referred to the last working crane tanks in the country which were to cease duty at Doxford's Shipyard in Pallion, Sunderland, on 29 January, 1971.

Crane tanks originated in the second half of the last century and were employed both in the works of main-line companies and in heavy industry where bulky and awkwardly shaped loads had to be handled. Over recent years such engines have been superseded by mobile cranes and fork-lift trucks. Commensurate with this, the Doxford crane tanks have long been regarded as important remnants from a past industrial age, and evidence of this is fully borne out by the fact that all four locomotives on the serviceable list in January, 1971 have since been purchased for private preservation.

The Doxford company have been important Wearside ship-builders since 1840 and are well known for their special design of Turret Ship. Over the years they have become noted for the construction of heavy derrick ships, destroyers and tank landing craft. During the 1960s the company achieved a unique distinction within Britain by building two 15,000-ton General cargo ships for Communist China and they are currently engaged in building a fleet of eight 16,800-ton cargo ships for Greece.

All basic materials necessary for the shipbuilding operations are delivered to Doxford's yard in sections/plates by rail, and the purpose of the company's internal railway system was to transfer these materials to various prefabrication shops in the shipyard. Furthermore the railway provided transport for heavy loads within the works and enabled prefabricated parts to be transferred from the various shops to the berths and fitting-out quays by the River Wear.

This method of operation commenced at the turn of the century when the yard was reconstructed to a layout based on the use of steam crane locomotives. Accordingly it was in 1902 that the first of these locomotives entered service. The original batch of five engines was built to Doxford's specifications by Hawthorn Leslie of Newcastle-upon-Tyne and they received names after various districts within the Sunderland area. Those commemorated were *Deptford, Wear, Hylton, Brownie* and *Pallion*; all were in service by 1904 but only the latter engine was destined to survive until 1971.

Due to the immense increase in shipbuilding concurrent with the outbreak of World War II, four further crane tanks were ordered from Robert Stephenson and Hawthorn, which was formed upon the merger of Hawthorn Leslie and Robert Stephenson Ltd. The original design of 1902 was perpetuated, the only difference being that steam brakes were fitted instead of handbrakes as on the original engines. In common with the earlier batch, the new engines were named after districts of Sunderland and the first two, in 1940, were named *Hendon* and *Roker* whilst *Millfield* and *Southwick* followed in 1942.

Apart from the basic locomotive design, the fascinating feature of these engines is of course the crane, which has a lifting capacity of 2 tons at 20′ radius, 3 tons at 15′ radius and 4 tons at 10′ radius. To facilitate operation of these different lengths, grappling hooks are situated at specified points along the jib. The jib lifting and swivel mechanism is completely separate from the main working of the loco and is self-contained in a housing on top of the fire-box. A tube from the boiler feeds this and a cylinder operates the rise and fall of the jib, while a crankshaft driving a worm, which in turn actuates a geared wheel on a turntable, revolves the crane. An unusual feature of the design is the mounting of the crane above the fire-box and not around the chimney or behind the footplate as is the usual practice.

The locomotives have 2 cylinders 12″ diameter × 15″ stroke, 2′ 10″ diameter driving wheels, a wheel base of 6′, a boiler pressure of 180 lb per sq in and a grate area of $9\frac{1}{2}$ sq ft. They weigh 24 tons. Other interesting features are the immense dumb buffers and modified Joy valve-gear. The Pallion workshops were responsible for the upkeep of the crane tanks and an interesting modification took place when the company rebuilt the boilers with 82 $1\frac{1}{2}$″ tubes instead of the original 120 $1\frac{3}{4}$″ ones. This allegedly improved the steaming qualities and gave a longer life to both the fire box and the smoke box tube plating. The locomotives' heating surface is 649 sq ft.

An immense pride was taken in the engines by the Doxford men and, as in most individualistic concerns, interested visitors were very warmly welcomed. In fact one gains the impression that the general wish within the company was for the locomotives to carry on indefinitely, but as time advanced the need for spare parts became a problem. After the absorption of Robert Stephenson and Hawthorn into the English Electric Co. in the 1950s all steam construction ceased and accordingly Doxfords attempted to prefabricate a welded fire-box when replacements became necessary. This was rejected by their insurance company as having too many welded seams but, because they lacked the plant, Doxfords were unable to remedy this. Furthermore track maintenance and running expenses over the 13 miles of track in the yard totalled over £20,000 p.a.; a fact that caused the company concern for some years! Even worse complications arose with the local council's intention, under the Clean Air Bill, to make Sunderland a smokeless zone. Tests made with the crane tanks burning smokeless fuel were unsatisfactory and it was found when using this material that the locomotives' firebars had very short lives.

Such factors forced the company into a decision to dispense with both the crane tanks and their railway network, and instead to lay roads over the rail beds and employ four new Scamell Trailer Lorries. This conversion was carried out gradually but by the end of 1970 only *Roker* and *Millfield* were in regular service, *Pallion* and *Southwick* were retained as standby engines and *Hendon* was withdrawn from service. Of the original batch, *Deptford* was scrapped in 1949, *Wear/Hylton* in 1952 and *Brownie* in 1968.

Once final closure of the system was agreed upon, scrap merchants delivered tenders to Doxfords for purchase of the crane tanks at a rate of £15 per ton. However in 1971 it would have been incomprehensible that such 'gems' should be allowed to pass into extinction and in fact no less than four of the remaining five were purchased for private preservation. *Millfield* was purchased for Bressingham Steam Museum, Norfolk, *Southwick* by Dinting Railway Centre and *Pallion* and *Roker* went to Goathland on the North Yorkshire Moors Railway. It is expected that apart from providing excellent interest at these centres the crane tanks will be able to earn their keep on track maintenance and general duties.

The story of the Doxford crane tanks has had a happy ending for when I made a special visit to film these engines in December, 1970 no preservation plans had been finalised. Certainly they will never be seen again within the confines of their exciting shipyard environment, but in any setting they constitute one of the most fascinating locomotive types preserved in Britain today and over the forthcoming years they will become the subject of very widespread interest.

C.P. Outside Cylinder 4–6–0 Nos 291–296   Pl. 59

These splendid machines of 1913 share the work along the Douro Valley line with their inside-cylinder relations of 1910 (see page 115), and although it may seem strange to affiliate genders with locomotives, these outside-cylinder engines always seem to be the masculine variety of the two types with their massive smoke deflectors, large cylinders and sharply angled footplating, all of which differ greatly from the more feminine lines of the 1910 engines. Built as a class of six engines by Henschel for the S.S. division of the Portuguese State Railways, they were originally used in the southern part of the country, but along with many other S.S. types, including the six inside-cylinder 4–6–0s, they were transferred to the north after modernisations on their native territory. It is fascinating that two sets of six 4–6–0s built for the same railway by the same builder within three years of one another should differ so greatly in appearance; and furthermore that both types should be working successfully side by side some 60 years later on a route completely different from that for which they were intended. The two types may be compared in plate numbers 58 and 59.

In the summer of 1971 the class remained intact and was shared between Régua and Contumil depots from which their light axle loading of $14\frac{1}{2}$ tons enabled them to work the Douro Valley line through to Barca d'Alva, and the Minho line up to Moncão. Although this light axle loading allows a wide route availability it does cause them to slip rather badly, especially when working some of the heavy mixed trains. Contumil and Régua are the only two broad-gauge steam depots in Portugal and the former, which handles the Minho line along with its various branches, is additionally responsible for engine repairs and major servicings, while Régua principally operates traffic through to the Spanish border at Barca d'Alva.

Despite their age these engines look surprisingly modern and are fine to see in action; their superb chime whistles have a penetrative quality which can be heard for many miles. They blend ideally with the Portuguese terrain whether rolling through the vineyards on the Minho line or working deep amid the Douro Valley's rugged bleakness. It is odd that this type seems to suit Portugal so well for it is not of any Portuguese descent and their lineage can hardly be said to include any national characteristics. The same applies   169 to all Portugal's steam engines which, beautiful though they are, have come from builders in far-away countries. I noticed especially the blending quality of these 4–6–0s whilst at Tua. It was evening and I was waiting for the westbound mixed train. The low-angle sun bathed the valley in different light tones giving the hills an air of loneliness and mystique. Looking over the river onto the hillside, on which the quiet hamlet of Tua is situated, I watched a villager trying to induce a donkey to pull a small plough; the obstinate beast proceeded for a few yards and for no apparent reason suddenly stopped, a process that was repeated continually until the man gave up. By this time my attentions had become diverted to the 4–6–0 approaching the viaduct with the mixed. It was then that I thought how well the class fitted into the Portuguese landscape. Plate no. 59 depicts this scene.

In common with the C.P.'s other broad-gauge engines, the class is oil-fired and it is this method of firing which produces the ecstatic clouds of smoke that are a present-day feature of Portuguese engines. I speak aesthetically and romantically when I say that these days there can be few scenes more exciting to a railway enthusiast than a 60-year-old 4–6–0 emitting shrouds of black smoke, with chime whistle blaring, and storming its way through some of Europe's wildest scenery. Such treasures are to be found on the Douro Valley line, a line that I would claim, unashamedly, to be perhaps the most exciting in Europe. The class has 2 cylinders $21\frac{1}{4}'' \times 26\frac{3}{4}''$, driving wheels of 5' 7'' diameter, a boiler pressure of 171 lb per sq in, a grate area of $32\frac{3}{4}$ sq ft, and a tractive effort of 23,095 lb. The total weight in working order is 113 tons.

D.B. 023 Class 2–6–2   Pl. 60

After the settlement of World War II, Germany's railways became divided, thus creating the West German 'Bundesbahn' (D.B.), and East German 'Reichsbahn' (D.R.). Despite the fact that many locomotives were given away as war reparations, the D.B. was not short of motive power. Pacifics were plentiful for the main passenger duties and there was a surplus of many kinds of 2–10–0 for freight work; in fact many of the 'Kriegsloks' (see page 128), especially those with plate frames which were troublesome to maintain, were dispensed with. A need that did exist, however, was for some medium-sized engines for general mixed traffic and special duties, though it was not until 1950 that the first of these, the 23 Class 2–6–2s, was introduced. In fact this class was the only one to be built in any quantity after the war; 105 were constructed between 1950 and 1959, by which time modernisation schedules curtailed all steam building.

These modern mixed-traffic engines, or 'Person-enzuglokomotive', were a development from the original Reichsbahn type 23, which first appeared in 1941. Only two of these were built initially, owing to standardisation of engines for war, and both passed to the East German D.R. after 1945, where over 100 more similar engines were built between 1956 and 1960. When the D.B. reintroduced the design many details had changed: the top feed dome disappeared, sand-boxes were removed from the boiler top, wing type smoke deflectors were fitted and the fascinating wide chimneys set a pattern for latter-day D.B. practice. The centre part of this chimney ejects exhaust from a single blast pipe in the normal way, whereas the exhaust passages of the air and feed-water pumps are fitted around the outside.

Perhaps the most notable characteristic of the 23s is their very high-pitched boilers. These enable the grate to clear both radial and rear coupled wheels and additionally allow considerable ease in maintenance. Earlier 23s had plain bearings, but the later ones, in accordance with much latter-day steam development, were fitted with roller-bearings. Their cab and tender are so designed to give drivers an uninterrupted view when the engines are working tender first, as they frequently do on single line and suburban services, whilst many, in common with the famous ex-Prussian P8s (D.B. 038 Class), are fitted for push-pull working. Actually, the original intention when designing the 23s was to use them as a replacement for the P8s, but subsequent modernisation plans thwarted this idea and until very recently the P8s have vastly outnumbered them.

An axle loading of $16\frac{3}{4}$ tons ensures the 23s of a wide route availability, but by altering the weight distribution, a maximum axle load of 19 tons can be obtained for service with heavy trains on suitable track. Other principal dimensions are: 2 cylinders $21\frac{1}{8}'' \times 26''$ driving wheels 5' $8\frac{1}{8}''$ diameter, boiler pressure 228 lb per sq in, and grate area $33\frac{1}{2}$ sq ft. The engine's weight in working order is 83 tons.

Today the 023s are well distributed throughout Western Germany and, at the time of writing, very few have been withdrawn. Their squat, rounded appearance gives them a unique character and they are by no means unpleasant looking. Possibly the greatest present-day concentration of them may be found in the Saarbrücken area where they work secondary passenger duties, though it is reasonable to assume that the class will be found in many parts of Western Germany for some years to come. One distinguished duty, held by them for a number of years, was working the *Rheingold* express from Venlo, on the Dutch border, to Cologne.

After World War I came the splitting up of the Austro-Hungarian Empire and one result of this was the formation of the Austrian Federal Railways, Ö.B.B., in 1923. This formation amalgamated the original State Railway with many independent companies though it was not until 1924, when the Ö.B.B. and Sudbahn merged, that Austria's railways finally became unified.

A wide variety of types were incorporated into the Ö.B.B.'s locomotive stock list, quite a percentage of which were part of the prolific output of Karl Gölsdorf, Chief Mechanical Engineer of the State Railway from 1891 to 1916, who, during that period, produced almost 50 separate designs. Gölsdorf was a great believer in compounding and, although essentially a 'big engine' man, he produced a series of diminutive 2-cylinder compound 2–6–0Ts for the State Railway. These engines, which later became the Ö.B.B. 91 Class, were built for passenger work over lightly-laid branches between 1897 and 1913. Variations occurred within their ranks, some engines having double-dome 'handle' boilers, while others possessed single domes but larger tanks and bunkers. In common with all Gölsdorf's early compounds these 2–6–0Ts have 2 cylinders: one high pressure of $14\frac{1}{2}''$ × $22\frac{1}{2}''$ and one low pressure of $22\frac{1}{2}''$ × $22\frac{1}{2}''$. Other specifications include driving wheels $3'\,7\frac{1}{4}''$ diameter, boiler pressure 185 lb per sq in, grate area 15 sq ft, and total weight in working order 40 tons. All locomotives were non-superheated.

Despite their antiquity, three of these delightful locomotives may still be found working from Mürzzuschlag, situated on the northern slopes of the Semmering line, where their duty is to operate passenger and mixed trains along the seven-mile branch to Neuberg. This picturesque line provides a wonderful piece of working history for it is a genuine country branch line worked by vintage steam engines – a tradition now almost entirely confined to the annals of history.

During our visit to the line, we followed the afternoon mixed train by road from Mürzzuschlag and having left the town we encountered a deep rural peace, our sinuous route affording us the finest joys of Austria's countryside. We easily kept up with the 2–6–0T which looked unbelievably quaint as it ran along the valleyside, its billows of fluffy white smoke flirting incessantly with the overhanging trees. The scene forcibly reminded me of the times when such rural treasures as this were commonplace in Britain. Before reaching Neuberg the train stopped to shunt, and the passenger coach was unceremoniously buffeted amid the clanking waggons, as if it were an empty truck instead of being full of country folk. With operations completed the little compound 2–6–0T summoned together its train and with a delightful scream from its whistle puffed away up the valleyside as one imagined it had done for the last seventy years. Rustic and antiquated, perhaps, but nevertheless a scene of such pure simplicity as to eternally endear it to one's heart.

Unfortunately, a diesel has encroached on to the branch, and inevitably this has taken away some of its character, but with a service of some eleven trains per day the 91s are usually well in evidence, and in fact, as late as August, 1971, I received news that during weekdays the line is often 100 per cent 91-worked. One can readily understand why the Neuberg branch has become a mecca for enthusiasts as without doubt it constitutes one of the principal attractions of present-day Austrian steam power. One of the engines is destined for preservation in the Austrian Railway Museum.

C.P. Metre Gauge Henschel 2–8–2T Nos E131–133   Pl. 87

This class of three engines was the first of Portugal's two metre-gauge 2–8–2T designs and was built by Henschel in 1924 to the requirements of the Val do Vouga Railway. The V.V. numbered them 31–33 but upon the company's absorption into the C.P. they were renumbered E131–33. They may still be found on the line for which they were built; all three are based at Sernada for operating trains between Espinho on the Atlantic coast and the beautiful cathedral city of Viseu. Heavy and powerful machines, they are ideally suited to the difficult terrain on this route and the class is a worthy forerunner of the later N.P. windshield-fitted 2–8–2Ts outlined on page 144. On the Sernada system they make a refreshing contrast with the many older and smaller engines although this set of 2–8–2Ts is considerably less modern-looking than their Henschel counterparts of 1931. One unique aspect of the class is the large ladders which extend down either side of the smoke-box to the top of the leading bogie wheels; one might imagine that these would impair the engines' appearance but in fact they do little to alter the heavy and squat outlines of the design.

The liveliness of these engines is remarkable, a fact borne out by our experiences one afternoon when we attempted, rather adventurously, to trail one on an afternoon train from Sernada to Viseu. The narrow valley roads were full of bends and other hazards; these we were prepared to contend with, but the sprightliness of the 2–8–2T was more than a match. The 2–8–2Ts whistle echoed tantalisingly across the wild valley always half a mile or so ahead of us and although we kept the train in sight for much of the journey there were several occasions when we rolled triumphantly into a station yard, cameras at the ready, only to find that the train had left. Such antics in the height of the Portuguese summer are calculated to daunt even the most jocular of spirits and having secured plate no. 87, we found that we had lost our enthusiasm to see the 2-8-2T arrive at Viseu; accordingly, having handed the laurels to the engine, we made a leisurely retreat back to Sernada to enjoy some of the less vivacious metre-gauge types.

Whilst discussing various metre-gauge locomotives in this volume I have made reference to their systems of origin, and some clarification of Portugal's metre-gauge history may be of interest. Originally the metre-gauge lines were owned by several independent concerns for in Portugal, before 1927, there was one large private company – the Portuguese Railway Company (C.P.) — smaller private companies and a number of state-owned lines. In 1927, however, the C.P. obtained a lease to operate all state-owned railways, thus acquiring much of the Portuguese metre-gauge network. Nevertheless, in 1928 it leased its metre-gauge lines to two independent companies: first the North of Portugal (N.P.), which was made up of both the Porto Póvoa and Famalicão Railway and the Guimarães Railway Co., and secondly the National Railways Co. (C.N.) This latter concern operated the various feeder lines in the Douro Valley, along with the Dão line. In 1947 the C.P. took control of all metre-gauge lines including the independent Val do Vouga Railway (V.V.) and all remain in unified form today along with the broad gauge (see page 155).

Ö.B.B. 78 Class 4-6-4T   Pl. 90

With the Gölsdorf era over, and the Austrian Railways in unified form, the 1920s/30s covered the final phase in the development of Austrian steam power. Further development of main-line passenger engines was slowed down because of impending electrification, and on the heavy freight side, ample Gölsdorf 0-10-0s/2-10-0s were in existence. In fact, after the Nazi occupation of Austria in 1938, when the Ö.B.B. became a part of the Deutsche Reichsbahn, D.R.B., the added introduction of various German 2-10-0s covered all freight engine requirements and no further designs were prepared.

However, developments were made with a range of standard tank engine classes, notable among which were batches of 4-6-2 (Ö.B.B. 77 Class), 4-6-4 (Ö.B.B. 78 Class) and 2-8-2 (Ö.B.B. 93 Class). Originally classified 729, the Ö.B.B. 78 4-6-4Ts are, excepting the Kriegsloks, the most modern steam engines in Austria today. The first series of 16 engines was built at Floridsdorf between 1931 and 1936, and a further ten were built under the German occupation in

1938/9; this latter batch had several Reichsbahn characteristics including inward-sloping cab sides.

These 2-cylinder simple engines are larger than their immediate forerunners, the 629 Class 4–6–2Ts of 1917, and were designed for hauling light, fast trains over short distances – a duty that they have performed to perfection. I have for long regarded the 78 Class as some of the most handsome tank engines ever built; they are majestic machines in every respect and their smoke deflectors add that final 'master touch'.

Aesthetics and excellence in performance however, do not make the sum total of the 78s' distinctions for, in the 1950s, one of them was chosen to be fitted with the original trial apparatus for Dr Giesl's superheater booster. The original stovepipe chimneys of the 78s had previously been replaced by Giesl ejectors and these, when combined with the superheater booster, increased the temperature of steam leaving the superheater from 337°C to 399°C. Such a difference resulted in a 20 per cent saving on coal consumption and so successful was the experiment that the Ö.B.B. decided to use it on all superheated, main-line engines despite the relative lateness of the innovation.

In view of the 78s' associations with Dr Giesl's inventions, and the use of the Giesl ejector upon other engines illustrated in this volume, perhaps it might be timely to make brief reference to this controversial, yet undoubtedly efficient, innovation. Dr Giesl himself was a designer on the staff of the Vienna Locomotive Works, Floridsdorf, and he was concerned by the fact that some two-thirds of the energy in exhaust steam is dissipated by 'shock loss' due to the difference in speed of the blastpipe steam and gases in the smoke-box. He concluded that the greatest suction for least exhaust steam was obtained by fitting multiple jets to exhaust the steam into a chimney many times longer than its width. The ejector reduced back pressure, increased superheat and, by reducing the shock loss, utilised much more of the kinetic energy of the exhaust. The net effect of this arrangement is to reduce fuel consumption and enable freer steaming. Apart from its widespread use in Austria, the Giesl ejector is to be found on locomotives the world over and it may be regarded as perhaps the last of the great technical developments made with the steam locomotive. Aesthetically it was a retrograde step, for apart from accentuating the angular starkness of certain designs, it disfigured the vast majority of locomotives upon which it was fitted. From this point of view it is fortunate that it was destined to remain as 'just another variety' in the myriad designs of locomotive chimneys.

However, the popularity with enthusiasts of the Giesl-fitted 78s is undisputed and the last survivors, which until recently were based at Amstetten, have been much sought after. Among their last duties was the operation of passenger trains 'under the wires' between Amstetten and Kleinreifling, due to a shortage of electric locomotives, although sometimes they continued on to Heiflau and Selzthal. In 1970 all surviving members of the class were transferred to Vienna for the operation of passenger trains between Praterstern and Bernhardsthal.

Leading dimensions of the class are: 2 cylinders $19\frac{5}{8}''$ × $28\frac{3}{8}''$, driving wheels 5' 2" diameter, boiler pressure 185 lb per sq in, grate area 38 sq ft and tractive effort 27,866 lb. Total weight in working order is 105 tons and the total adhesive weight of $46\frac{1}{2}$ tons is light for so powerful a machine.

With only a handful remaining in traffic and there being little likelihood of these receiving anything more than light repairs, it seems almost certain that 1972 will see these fascinating engines pass to extinction. However, one is stored at Linz shed for intended inclusion in the Austrian Railway Museum and a splendid exhibit it will eventually make.

Hunslet 16" 0–6–0ST Pl. 93, 94

The Hunslet Engine Company has for long been one of Britain's most important private locomotive builders; their designs have infiltrated into all sections of British industrial railways and furthermore they are to be found throughout the world on both main-line and industrial systems.

The locomotive illustrated is an example of the famous 16" Hunslet Saddle Tanks of 1923, one of that company's standard designs and a forerunner of the ubiquitous 'Austerities' (see page 136). Large numbers were built and they have become a familiar sight among British industrial systems; so popular were they in fact that Hunslet were still receiving orders for them in the late 1950s – over thirty years after the original engines appeared!

Their typical haunts have been collieries, ironstone mines and power stations. Furthermore they have been extensively used by Guest, Keen and Baldwin of Cardiff and the Austin Motor Works at Longbridge. Quite a number still remain in service and they are one of the most distinctive designs still to be found in British industry. They have 2 cylinders 16" × 22", a boiler pressure of 160 lb per sq in and driving wheels of 3' 9" diameter.

The plates show two of these engines performing a duty of considerable significance and one which has led to their both being preserved. The engines, named *Jacks Green* and *Ring Haw,* belonged to the Nassington Barrowden Mining Co. and until closure of the Nassington system early in 1971 they were the last steam engines to work on British ironfields. To add to Nassington's distinction of being a final stronghold of steam power, it should be noted that the entire ironstone industry has been developed around the steam locomotive. Indeed, it was the advent of steam power in the early 19th century that led to the vast exploitation of Britain's mineral wealth. For well over a century, steam locomotives were employed on ironfields but, due to a decline in demand for British iron-ore and modernisations within the industry, the final moments were played out by these Hunslet 0–6–0STs in January, 1971. In view of its historical importance, Nassington attracted many visitors and in its latter days it became almost a foregone conclusion that both locomotives would be preserved; no other engines of this type had been saved previously.

Jacks Green was purchased by the Peterborough Locomotive Society for £900 and, upon the cessation of mineral working at Nassington, ran under its own steam to its temporary base at the British Sugar Corporation, Peterborough. During the course of this journey it achieved yet another unique distinction: that of running live over B.R. metals in 1971 – no mean feat indeed! The Peterborough Locomotive Society has delivered a report to the Peterborough Development Council outlining plans for a section of the Nene Valley line to be retained for recreational activities and, if successful, services might be extended to Nassington itself. It was with this scheme in mind that *Jacks Green* was purchased, and accordingly it is possible that the famous mining area of Nassington might once again resound to the barking exhaust of a 16″ Hunslet 0–6–0ST.

After the completion of demolition work at Nassington in mid-February, *Ring Haw* also made the journey under her own steam to the British Sugar Corporation, Peterborough where, on the same day she was put onto a low loader for transfer by road to the North Norfolk Railway at Sheringham. During the first part of the journey *Ring Haw* was still in steam, to the utter incredulity of roadside viewers!

The story of these two locomotives was covered in my earlier book, *Symphony in Steam* (Blandford), and by any standards their story is a lovely one. It is most fitting that both have been preserved and now it will be possible for these two veterans of the pits to be enjoyed by future generations.

D.B. 078 Class 4–6–4T   Pl. 95
The Neckar Valley in Germany's Black Forest region has become one of the final haunts of this once prolific and distinguished class of tank engine, and the saying that 'handsome is as handsome does' well befits these ex-Prussian

177

veterans. Between 1912 and 1927 almost 500 were constructed, many by the Vulkan Naval Yards at Stettin. Originally they were classified T18 by the Prussians (later D.B. 078), the 'T' designation applying to 'Tenderlokomotive' or Tank Engine: in fact the class may be regarded as a tank engine version of the famous Prussian P8 Class 4–6–0s.

Initially, the T18s were introduced for operation on the Hesse lines between the terminals of Frankfurt and Wiesbaden and their introduction obviated the need for tender engines which were uneconomical on these services. Having proved themselves on general suburban and short distance work, the T18s were widely adopted by the D.R.B. and reclassified 78^{0-10}. Due to the intense standardisation policy of the D.R.B., shortly after its inception in 1920, very few pre-nationalisation types survive today. Accordingly the 078s, along with a handful of 055s (ex-Prussian G8 0–8–0) and 038s (ex-Prussian P8 4–6–0s), remain on today's D.B. as working testimonials to the rich locomotive history of Germany.

Fortunately, Western Germany is not the only country to retain the T18s, for after World War I, the newly independent state of Poland, much of whose territory had been in Prussia, inherited many Prussian locomotives. This had a considerable influence upon subsequent locomotive development in that country and in 1927 a batch of T18s was built for Poland. These became classified 0Kol, some of which remain at work today. In addition, many Prussian locomotives were drafted into Turkey during World War I, and after the unification of the Turkish railways in 1927, some ex-Prussian types were built for the new administration. Principally, these were G10 0–10–0s and $G8^2$ 2–8–0s, but a batch of eight T18s was included. These T18s were built in Germany by Henschel for working the Haydarpasa suburban trains and some still remain in service on today's Turkish State Railways.

The leading dimensions of the 078s are: 2 cylinders $22'' \times 24\frac{1}{8}''$, driving wheels of 5' 5'' diameter, boiler pressure 171 lb per sq in and a grate area of 26 sq ft. In common with their forerunners, the P8s, all 078s were superheated and their total weight in full working order is 106 tons.

As recently as the mid-1960s some three hundred 078s were in operation in Western Germany, but since then their numbers have diminished rapidly and in 1971 only a few survived, all in the Stuttgart region of Southern Germany. Their final workings include trains from Rottweil, where they are based, to Tuttlingen, Tübingen and Villingen; it was during the operation of these services that the colour plate was obtained. The 078s cannot survive for much longer (though which of the three countries concerned will be the last to retain their services is uncertain at the time of writing), but until their final demise, they will continue to be one of the most interesting locomotive types on the continent of Europe. One example is set by for preservation and this engine is at Schwerte in Western Germany.

Ö.B.B. 93 Class 2-8-2T   Pl. 99

The 1920/30s were the final phase of development in Austrian steam power, and were mainly devoted to building a range of standard tank engines, because the requirement for main-line passenger engines were somewhat diminished by the growth of electrification. In 1927 the Austrian Federal Railway introduced two noteworthy standard designs: the 392 Class 0-8-0 shunting tanks (originally Class 478), and the 93 Class 2-8-2 tanks for secondary line services (originally Class 378). Standard parts included: boiler, motion, axleboxes, wheel centres and water tanks. Extra wheels, provided on the 93s, were necessary in order to keep the individual axle load down to 11 tons – a restriction not applying to the shunting engine on which a maximum of 16 tons per axle was permitted. Owing to the lessened adhesion weight of 44 tons on the 93s, against 64 tons on the 392s, the former were fitted with slightly smaller cylinders.

The 93s are rugged, powerful and efficient and have been successfully employed on secondary services in many parts of Austria for almost fifty years. Gradients of 1 in 40 are tackled with 200-ton trains, and the class is allocated a maximum speed of 50 m.p.h. Of the first 100 93s to be built, fifty came from the Floridsdorf Locomotive Construction Co. of Vienna and fifty from the Austro-Hungarian State Railway Works, also in Vienna.

Principal dimensions are: 2 cylinders $17\frac{3}{4}'' \times 22''$, boiler pressure 199 lb per sq in, driving wheels 3' $7\frac{1}{4}''$ diameter and a grate area of 22 sq ft. Other features are the incorporation of Lentz Poppet Valves and Schmidt Superheating, along with a coal and water capacity of almost 3 tons and 2,200 gallons respectively. Twenty-five engines of the same design, but with detailed variations, were put into service by Czechoslovakia between 1942 and 1944 and became that country's 431 Class.

Unlike their sister engines, the 392 Class, which is now virtually extinct, the 93s have become the most numerous tank locomotives in Austria, and as late as 1971 some seventy were still on the active list. Thirty-five of these were assigned to Mistelbach for operating the network of secondary services north of Vienna. Their design is rather angular, and by fitting Giesl ejectors to the majority of the class a rather excitingly grotesque effect has been obtained. This effect is highlighted in plate no. 99. One fascinating feature of the class is the ash-chutes which protrude out onto the framing from a small door built into the smoke-box bottom. This device obviates the need to open the smoke-box door when clearing ashes.

Although steam power is responsible for only a small percentage of traffic in present-day Austria, with fewer than 350 engines remaining in 1971, it appears that it will be extant for some time yet, especially since some engines have recently received important overhauls, and almost certainly amongst the engines that survive, albeit in ever dwindling numbers, will be some of these splendid 93 Class 2–8–2Ts.

Hawthorn Leslie 0–6–0ST   Rear Endpaper

Although January, 1971 saw the last steam locomotives disappear from Northamptonshire's ironfields, a remarkable pocket of steam – one of the largest remaining in British industrial use – survived until the summer of 1971 at the British Steel Corporation's Corby Works. These works originally belonged to Stewart and Lloyds Ltd and are part of a vast system of mining, smelting and steel tube-making which has grown up in the heart of Northamptonshire's ore-beds. The adjacent ironstone mines are connected to the steel works by one of Britain's most complex industrial railway systems, and it was amid this hive of industry that the pocket of steam engines remained. Corby Works has an annual steel-making capacity of one million tons and at night the glow of the furnaces can be seen for miles across the undulating countryside.

In 1932 an immense expansion programme was undertaken at Corby Works, a development which was a first step in turning Corby from a village of some 1,500 inhabitants to the sprawling steel town that it is today. Accordingly, Stewart and Lloyds ordered six new 16″ Hawthorn Leslie 0–6–0STs to cope with the extra traffic and these engines, which were delivered in 1934, were based on the successful use of a similar engine dated 1919, acquired by Stewart and Lloyds from the North Lincolnshire Ironstone Co. in 1931. Once firmly established as the standard steelworks locomotive, four more were ordered from Hawthorn Leslie in 1936, along with a further one in 1938, while the final two, delivered during an expanded steel production in World War II, came in 1940 and 1941 to the original Hawthorn Leslie design, from Robert Stephenson and Hawthorn. This company formed on the merger between Hawthorn Leslie and Robert Stephenson Co. Ltd.

For some years these engines, with one exception, were solely responsible for the steam operations around Corby

Works. The exception was a survivor of Hunslet's 18″ 50550 Class (see page 136), which was built at Stewart and Lloyd's request for their intended Islip Orefield Development. Although eight were built, Stewart and Lloyd's abandonment of the Islip project meant that only one was ever destined to work at Corby and this, surprisingly enough, went to the steel works where, despite being an 'odd man out' it was useful for some of the heavier jobs such as working hot iron ladles between the blast furnaces and steel-making plants.

In order to be seen amongst the gloomy works surroundings, the fourteen Hawthorn Leslies adopted a livery of buttercup yellow and some had additional black and yellow dazzle striping on their saddle tank fronts and buffers. Their leading dimensions are: 2 outside cylinders 16″ × 24″, boiler pressure 180 lb per sq in and driving wheels 3′ 8″ diameter. The engines are $28\frac{1}{2}′$ long, 12′ high and $8\frac{1}{2}′$ wide and their approximate weight is 33 tons.

When built, the Hawthorn Leslies were traditional coal-burners but in 1960, owing chiefly to a shortage of suitable coal, Stewart and Lloyds adopted a plan of oil-firing. After an initial experiment, half the class were fitted over the following three years.

This oil-burning system was devised at Corby Works and consisted of a burner mounted in the ash-pan bottom. Two separately-controlled steam distributors were necessary for activating the oil in the fire-box, one to atomise the fuel upon entry, the other to jet-spray it around the fire-box. Before these engines could be lit, steam pressure had to be available for initial atomisation, and this was done either from a reduced works supply at 50 lb per sq in, connected through a flexible pipe to the control fitting, or alternatively by the use of compressed air.

Apart from overcoming the coal problem, these engines had a number of additional advantages, principally increased locomotive availability, as steam could be raised within one hour whereas three hours had been necessary with coal. Furthermore, no fire-cleaning or bunkering-up was necessary. Conversely, however, one distinct disadvantage was that if the engines were left unattended for long periods their boiler pressures fell rapidly. Another difficulty arose in the possibility of scrap which lay between the tracks damaging the oil-burning equipment mounted on the ashpan, and, in view of this, oil-burners were not preferred on certain duties. It is interesting to note that it was this very problem which decided the company to use outside-cylinder engines upon steelworks duties, because the internal mechanisms of inside-cylinder locomotives would be vulnerable in exactly the same way. Notwithstanding this, the oil-burners were interesting and success- 181 ful engines and could immediately be recognised by their slightly enlarged coal bunkers in which were fitted the 600-gallon oil supply tanks. The locomotive illustrated is, however, a traditional coal-burner.

The very nature of Corby Works ensured that visits there were dramatic and moving experiences so one could hardly say that the Hawthorn Leslies animated their settings, but they did blend with them wonderfully, and added a distinctive touch of character to the works environment. Their thin piping whistles were an intrinsic part of life at the works – with the exception of one engine which succeeded in procuring a chime whistle! Endlessly active around the works, these little engines were enthralling to watch as they rumbled from plant to plant. Round past the fiery blast furnaces, amid the smouldering coke-ovens, down amid the clamour of the tube works or storming along with loads of raw materials and steel tubes, it was all part of their day. Here was true industry, and here was the Hawthorn Leslies' world.

Tragically, the end came during 1971 with the arrival of five English Electric six-coupled, diesel-hydraulic engines, and so ended the saga of Corby's yellow Hawthorn Leslies – the last steam engines on the Lincolnshire–Oxfordshire iron-stone belt. By good fortune one of the first engines to be withdrawn was purchased by Mr Hunt of Hunt's Mineral Waters, Hinckley, Leicestershire for private preservation, and in the summer of 1971 he declared to me his intention to purchase two more with a view to future operation in preserved form. Another member of the class is earmarked for purchase by Corby Urban District Council for installation as a children's attraction at Corby's West Glebe Park, although has consideration been given to placing it in the town centre, in its original livery, as an historic relic. It is to be fervently hoped that this latter idea is put in hand, as a children's playground is hardly the most suitable place to erect so noble a monument to the iron-steam partnership that made Corby what it is today – a steel town of some 50,000 inhabitants.

Index

Cross reference between colour plates and text pages